D0844796

Twayne's English Authors Series

EDITOR OF THIS VOLUME

Kinley E. Roby

Northeastern University

Sheila Kaye-Smith

TEAS 278

Camera Portrait by E. O. Hoppe

Sheila Kaye–Smith

SHEILA KAYE-SMITH

By DOROTHEA WALKER

*Nassau Community College,
State University of New York*

TWAYNE PUBLISHERS
A DIVISION OF G. K. HALL & CO., BOSTON

Copyright © 1980 by G. K. Hall & Co.

Published in 1980 by Twayne Publishers,
A Division of G. K. Hall & Co.

Printed on permanent / durable acid-free paper and bound
in the United States of America

First Printing

Library of Congress Cataloging in Publication Data

Walker, Dorothea.
Sheila Kaye-Smith.

(Twayne's English authors series ; TEAS 278)
Bibliography: p. 163–66
Includes index.
1. Kaye-Smith, Sheila, 1887–1956—
Criticism and interpretation
PR6021.A8Z95   823'.9'12   79–16671
ISBN 0–8057–6777–0

To Ray,
with admiration—
with gratitude—
with love.

Contents

About the Author
Preface
Acknowledgments
Chronology
1. Early Life and Influences   17
2. Impetus to Being: Convergence
   of Inner and Outer   27
3. Struggling Women   56
4. Later Life and Later Novels   85
5. Religion and Family   94
6. The Matter of Class   124
7. Final Estimate   152
   Notes and References   155
   Selected Bibliography   163
   Index   167

About the Author

Dorothea Walker is a professor of English at Nassau Community College, State University of New York, where she teaches courses in women's studies, literature, and writing. Professor Walker holds the A.B. degree from Hunter College, City University of New York and the M.A. and Ph.D. degrees from St. John's University, Hillcrest, New York.

Professor Walker has published a Twayne United States Authors book on Alice Brown, a New England writer. She has also published articles and book reviews on women's studies and American literature.

Professor Walker is active in affirmative action. She developed the first women's studies course in the English Department of her college, and she continues to teach it. Active in the Women's Faculty Association and the National Organization of Women, she conducts workshops and seminars, working constantly toward the attainment of full equality for women.

Preface

Looking at ideas supplied by critics, one finds that Sheila Kaye-Smith appears as a novelist of Sussex, a convert to Catholicism, a woman who writes like a man. As her work spans a period of nearly fifty years (*The Tramping Methodist*, 1908, to *The View from the Parsonage*, 1954) much of the assessment of her work resides in articles and reviews written by men or written by women following masculine prejudice on what good writing reveals. It is extremely doubtful that a woman writer would be praised today for having a "masculine" mind.

Critics who point to her conversion from Methodism through Anglo-Catholicism to Roman Catholicism dwell on the religious aspects they find in her work and attempt to correlate these with her spiritual progress. The third group, those who emphasize her realism in using Sussex for locale and character, point out the verity of the presentation, even to actual names, places, and dialect.

All of these observations, of course, are interesting and enlightening and help the reader to find, perhaps, an extra dimension to the very good story told by Sheila Kaye-Smith. I do not mean to imply that there is not some analysis of plot, style, and character present in the critical material, but in general, emphasis focuses on the three major areas mentioned above.

This study, the first book length analysis of the novels of Sheila Kaye-Smith, centers on a different aspect of her work. This aspect is the artistic vision which reveals to the reader an emotional understanding of some of the deepest needs of human beings. In presenting characters caught up in, and responding to, these needs, Sheila Kaye-Smith gains an added dimension, for she helps the reader to understand not only the cause and effect of the plight of her characters, but also the cause and effect of many of the problems of human beings as they make their climb to maturity. And the understanding may lead to some regard for the mystery that she sees as the center of life. Events of her life amplify and support her vision, and I have included significant ones which help the reader of the novels to gain some insight into their author's mind.

Thus, this study centers on Sheila Kaye-Smith's vision of life as a whole, rather than on that of a particular society of a particular time, although the novelist did not ignore the effect of cultural and political ideas when they suited her story. As she wrote her novels, she told different stories. The aim of this study is to analyze the most significant of these only, even though all have importance and interest for the reader. Sheila Kaye-Smith knows how to tell a good story. The emphasis of this study is to get beyond the story and into the understanding of human nature and of human values that the story enfolds.

Although it is difficult to explain precisely the literary influences which formed Sheila Kaye-Smith's matter and manner of presentation in her novels, it can be noted that she followed Fanny Burney in her novels of manners as well as Maria Edgeworth in her family history chronicles and Sir Walter Scott in his attempt to go back into the past, even so far as racial memory. She may also be likened to Jane Austen in that her heroines are always honest in their attitude toward love, a far cry from the dishonest attitudes found in heroines of most of the novels by women novelists of the time. She is certainly outside of the sentimentality of most of the cloying Victorian women writers (although it must be admitted that some of her very early novels exhibit some of this sentimentality). Like Thomas Hardy and Rudyard Kipling, she finds the countryside a powerful influence on the lives of people, and she writes always with her idea of this influence both dictating the kind of life her characters lead and forcing them into decisions through which self emerges. Her readership extends outside the purely feminine one, as critical acclaim at a time when women writers were considered far inferior to men writers pays her the then highest compliment—the compliment that she "writes like a man."

In selecting novels for analysis, I have been guided by critical acclaim only insofar as it mirrored my own assessment. I have also been guided by my desire to show similarities and differences in the manner of approach and the point of view of the various novels selected, as this illustrates Miss Kaye-Smith's artistry and her inventive power, as well as her ability to view from various angles. I have selected powerful novels, in the hope that a novelist who once enjoyed great popularity and critical acclaim may be rescued from that near obscurity which has been the fate of too many excellent women novelists. At the present time, when women are resurrecting their past, and with it those lost artists of the past, it seems fitting that Sheila Kaye-Smith's vision, presented with genuine literary talent, should again be held up to public view, to enchant a new generation of readers.

I have presented facts of Miss Kaye-Smith's life primarily so that the reader might better understand her work. Much of this background material comes from her own autobiography. It is my wish that the reader of this study will enjoy making, or renewing, an acquaintance with Sheila Kaye-Smith. More important, I hope that the reader will grow to a better self-awareness through experiencing her vision, as I have.

I would like to express my appreciation to the Nassau Community College Library, particularly to Professor Emanuel Finkel for his invaluable aid in obtaining out-of-print books and critical material and to Professor Aurelia Stephan for her expert assistance in searching out hard-to-find facts. I would like, also, to thank the librarians at Hofstra University, Hempstead, New York, and the New York Public Library at Forty-second Street, New York, for their courteous and valuable service.

I wish to express my special gratitude to Professor Paul A. Doyle of Nassau Community College, not only for his outstanding bibliography of Sheila Kaye-Smith, which made my work possible, but also for his suggestion that this book be written and his kindness in reading it in manuscript. I am deeply in his debt for pointed criticism and suggestions, as well as for his never failing lively interest during the often frustrating periods of research and writing.

Finally, I thank my colleagues and friends at Nassau Community College for their helpful advice and firm support, not only in recognizing the value of a study such as this, but in granting me the necessary sabbatical leave to complete the work.

DOROTHEA WALKER

Nassau Community College
State University of New York
Garden City, Long Island

Acknowledgments

I wish to express my gratitude to the following for permission to quote from copyrighted material:

To Harcourt Brace Jovanovich, Inc. for permission to quote from Introduction to *Hour of Gold, Hour of Lead* by Anne Morrow Lindbergh.

To the New York Public Library for permission to quote from John D. Gordan, *Novels in Manuscript: An Exhibition from the Berg Collection* (The New York Public Library 1965). Reprinted with permission.

To Charles Scribner's Sons for permission to quote from Lionel Trilling, *The Liberal Imagination.*

To *The Times Literary Supplement* (London) for permission to quote from "The Old Forest," *The Times Literary Supplement* (London), November 13, 1953.

To the University of North Carolina Press for permission to quote from James W. Tuttleton, *The Novel of Manners in America.*

Chronology

1887   February 4: Sheila Kaye-Smith born in Hastings, Sussex, daughter of a country doctor.

1896–   Attended Hastings and St. Leonards Ladies' College.
1905

1905–   Wrote for magazines such as *Pearson's Weekly, Hastings*
1929   *Advertiser, Everyman, Storyteller, Harper's Magazine, Ladies' Home Journal.*

1908   *The Tramping Methodist.*

1909   *Starbrace.*

1910   *Spell Land.*

1911   Took trip to Paris. *Samuel Richardson.*

1913   *Isle of Thorns.*

1914   *The Three Furlongers (Three Against the World). Willows Forge and Other Poems.*

1916   *Sussex Gorse. John Galsworthy.*

1917   *The Challenge to Sirius.*

1918   Received into the Anglican Church. *Little England.*

1919   *Tamarisk Town.*

1920   *Green Apple Harvest.*

1922   *Joanna Godden.*

1923   *The End of the House of Alard. Saints in Sussex.*

1924   Married Reverend F. Penrose Fry, Anglican Rector at St. Leonards-on-Sea. Moved to London. *The George and the Crown.*

1925   *The Mirror of the Months.*

1926   *Joanna Godden Married* (a volume of short stories).

1928   Took cruise to Italy with her husband. *Iron and Smoke.*

1929   Converted to the Roman Catholic Church. Moved to "Little Doucegrove," a small farm in Sussex. *The Village Doctor.*

1929–   Performed religious works of mercy as a clergyman's
1956   wife might have done.

1930   *Shepherds in Sackcloth.* Mass said at Little Doucegrove for the first time, publicly, since the Reformation.

1931 *Late and Early* (a volume of poetry). *Susan Spray.*
1933 *Gipsy Waggon. The Children's Summer.*
1934 *Superstition Corner. Gallybird.*
1935 *Selina (Selina Is Older).*
1936 *Rose Deeprose.*
1937 *Three Ways Home.*
1938 *The Valiant Woman.*
1940 *Ember Lane.*
1942 *The Secret Son (The Hidden Son).*
1943 *Tambourine, Trumpet, and Drum.*
1945 *Kitchen Fugue.*
1947 *Joanna Godden* made into a motion picture.
1948 *The Lardners and the Laurelwoods.*
1949 *The Happy Tree.*
1951 *Mrs. Gailey.*
1954 *The View from the Parsonage.*
1956 Died at her home on January 14. *All the Books of My Life.*

CHAPTER 1

Early Life and Influences

POSSIBLY Sheila Kaye-Smith's father would not have taken the hyphen had he not married her mother, a de la Condamine who had had "till the end of her life an unutterable contempt of Smith. Nothing annoyed her more than when . . . Kaye was dropped or taken for a mere initial." Miss Kaye-Smith states flatly that she "cannot pretend that [the] hyphen was not mainly snobbish in origin and intention," for her mother "was a snob."[1] Undoubtedly Miss Kaye-Smith's intimate acquaintance with snobbery laid the foundation for her interest in this psychological need, for she probes its depth in many of her novels, notably *The Lardners and the Laurelwoods* and *Mrs. Gailey.*

Of the Smith side of her father's family, Miss Kaye-Smith knew very little, surmising that the family was not a very notable one. The children of the Kaye-Smith union either dropped the Smith or took the hyphen, as Sheila's father did. On his mother's side there was a brother, Sir John Kaye, a historian and writer. His *History of the Indian Mutiny* became a textbook for army cadets, but his one or two novels passed into oblivion. The Kayes, a Lincolnshire family, were from the squire class, closely allied with the Church of England. They supplied the church with several dignitaries. Sheila Kaye-Smith recalls that when she first saw Bishop Kaye lying on his tomb in Lincoln Cathedral, she immediately noticed his resemblance to her father, as her father had appeared a few hours after his death.[2]

Miss Kaye-Smith's mother's family differed in country and religion from her father's, having left France in the eighteenth century and come to the Channel Islands as Huguenot refugees. Miss Kaye-Smith reveals that "one Sunday they all did public penance in the Town Church for having returned to their vomit—in other words, for having attended Mass while on a holiday in France."[3]

When Robert de La Condamine, Sheila's grandfather, married a Miss MacFarquhar, no French was spoken in the house, and Robert embraced Presbyterianism, giving up Protestant Anglicanism. Thus Sheila's mother remained Presbyterian in sympathy, although she outwardly conformed to the Church of England after she married Sheila's father.

To this union of Kaye-Smith and de la Condamine, Sheila was born on February 4, 1887. Her father, a son of an army surgeon and himself a doctor, was born in India. Sheila was born in Hastings, in Sussex, and was, then, "the child of opposites, having on one side all that is solid, English and Anglican . . . and on the other a rather volatile mixture of Scottish and French, Celt and Latin, Presbyterian and Huguenot (with Catholic cravings, if one is to judge by that French holiday)."[4]

It is important to note Miss Kaye-Smith's ancestry and background, including her childhood, as she, herself, feels that "an author is conditioned by the time he is twelve." And she feels that it is certainly "the first twelve years of [her] life that made [her] a Sussex novelist."[5] As to what made her a Roman Catholic, she who was the product of Low Church parents, she attributes it to "two words—God's Grace." She adds that she has never really changed her religion, having "always been latently and potentially a Catholic—there has been no swing round from a contradictory set of ideas."[6]

The story of her change from the religion of her parents through Anglo-Catholicism to Roman Catholicism appears in *Three Ways Home,* published in 1937. It is not the burden of this study to follow this change. "High" Church values are ordinarily seen as superior to "Low," particularly in church liturgy, in her novels, but the novels themselves do not carry the burden of religious tracts. That religion informed her life and interest may be seen in her many presentations of clergymen and itinerant preachers. But it is *religion* (values connected with God) which overrides her ideas, rather than any apology for a specific religion. She sought her own truth, and she found it in Roman Catholicism.

In addition to religious influences, the lifestyle of her family, who lived in St. Leonards, a seaside resort of Hastings (and immortalized in *Tamarisk Town),* gave her both the security to develop and the matter from which to draw her stories. Her father was a busy doctor, and Sheila often accompanied him on his rounds. *The Village Doctor* (1929), which went through at least seventeen printings and was selected as Dutton's Book of the Month, reveals a knowledge and authenticity, and an affection, which could only have been drawn from experience.

I *Childhood*

Her affection for her father underlies the picture of Selina's father in the two autobiographical novels based on her childhood, *The Children's Summer* (1932) and *Selina* (1935). "In only one matter did Selina hold that she and Moira had a decided advantage over their new friends, and that was in the matter of fathers. She would rather wear white socks and go to bed at six all her life than to exchange her own father, so tall and strong and kind and clever, for Mr. Clifford."[7] Although the mother appears in brief glimpses in these novels, it remains the father who understands and comforts.

Added to St. Leonards as matter for her novels were the farms the children stayed at during the summer, Platnix in particular. Here the children played with farmers' children and envied them their freedom from the restrictions of children in upper class Victorian society. The story of Selina and her sister, Moira, which is the story of Sheila Kaye-Smith and her sister, presents a charming, loving father and a gay, affectionate mother, both giving strength and moral support to two little girls whose physical care is completely in the hands of a nurse. Nurse represents stability, so much so that the little girls are adversely affected more by her departure to take care of a family problem than they are by the departure of their parents for a vacation.

The growth of the imagination, the stirrings of religious questioning, the touch of mysticism—all appear in these stories based on Miss Kaye-Smith's childhood, and the combination charms.[8]

Along with her joy in the glorious summers at Platnix and at other farms, Sheila delighted in telling stories. She seems to have been born with this desire, which never left her. When only three years old, she made believe she was reading out of a book as she walked around her parents' bedroom, entertaining them as they drank early morning tea. Later, after her marriage, while walking in the country with her husband, she would suddenly start telling him a story.[9] She is undoubtedly the Selina to whom "learning to write made much more difference . . . than learning to read. . . . Selina often said to herself: As soon as I can write I shall write my own stories."[10] For that is what Sheila Kaye-Smith did.

Gladys Stern (hereafter referred to as G. B. Stern) feels that both *The Children's Summer* and *Selina* "provide a vivid blueprint for her whole career in theological adventure: the embryonic author, too, is seen making significant discoveries— ('Mother, can you eggsplain something? Why is it that when I write a play it's different to what was in my mind, and when I act it it's still more different')."[11] This embryonic writer "composed forty-two novels in her head" and wrote out thirteen more during her last two years at school.[12] Some of this material appears in her first two published novels, *The Tramping Methodist* (1908) and *Starbrace* (1909).

Her writing was spontaneous. W. Gore Allen, writing in the *Irish Ecclesiastical Record,* refers to her "ancestral springs of great achievement; somewhere Highland blood, intermarried with the French; and these very Frenchmen sufficiently alive to be persecuted by professionally Catholic politicians; then—safe in a Protestant society—to be publicly rebuked because they showed a hungering for Mass; somewhere wedded bliss in face of class distinction; somewhere an officer in India who spent his spare time writing novels."[13] She herself admits: "When I began to write I could find within myself all the material I needed, bright with the star-dust with which the unconscious gilds even the dullest gingerbread."[14] Edward Wagenknecht agrees that in her "early days, Miss Kaye-Smith wrote intuitively; when she could no longer do this, she felt that her work began to fail; it was not until *Rose Deeprose* (1936) that she could believe herself to be achieving a blend of 'thought and instinct, conscious and unconscious.' "[15]

Before going on to her later development, one must mention her education. Starting at nine years of age, she attended, for nine years, Hastings and St. Leonards Ladies' College, which was located a few steps from her home. This study comprised her formal education. The mistresses of this academy had no degrees, but they were women of culture and intelligence who had "the priceless gift of making lessons interesting," so that the young Sheila was never bored and felt that "learning was less of a rod than a wand waved lightly" over her. Her school prizes were books. When she was old enough, she was allowed to choose her own prizes. She chose Milton's *Collected Poems* and Dante's *Divine Comedy*.[16] One can surmise, both from her choice of books and from the fact that the mistresses were "women of culture and intelligence" that the education of the young author was excellent indeed.

From her own account, Miss Kaye-Smith had "what everyone would call a happy childhood, with a comfortable home, kind parents and many friends."[17] Her childhood dreams centered on her determination to be a writer, to "live alone in a little cottage on the land between Westfield and Sedlescome. . . . be a celebrated author whose novels of rural life were famous throughout the world . . . and be extremely High Church."[18]

As she achieved her dreams, her life story is that of the anatomy and growth of a novelist and the groping of a religious nature to end in Roman Catholicism. Her heritage, her family, her childhood, and her surroundings all gave their gifts to her imagination and to her natural skill. She fulfilled her dream of becoming a celebrated author; she also fulfilled her dream of becoming "extremely High Church" through her conversion to Roman Catholicism. She regarded both of these as central to her life. How the first dream became a reality may be seen by examining her early novels.

II *Early Novels*

Sheila Kaye-Smith's first published novel, *The Tramping Methodist* (1908), took her just under a year to write. She was twenty-one. Because she was "pleased with the work on the whole, but . . . felt diffident about certain parts and longed for expert advice," she sent the manuscript to the Reading Branch of the Society of Authors. She fixed the pen name E. C. Ticehurst to the manuscript, out of the "desire to be taken for a man." However, the society's reader advised her to use her own name, and much encouraged by the "detailed criticism," which aided her to remove glaring crudenesses, and his assessment that it was good enough to send to a publisher, she sent it to The Literary Agency of London.[19]

Her religious convictions at this time "sank into that borderland between religion and superstition where prayer is only the voice of a greedy child crying Gimme . . . Gimme . . . I want . . . I want . . . I want *The Tramping Methodist* to be published. Please, God, make somebody publish *The Tramping Methodist.*"[20] She had given up her High Church ambitions, as her parents disapproved of them and forbade her to go to the local High Church or to join any of its societies. The unfulfilled desire for a High Church religion tormented her to the extent that when she gave it up, she thereby gave up much of religion itself. She states that her religious life, "over-sublimated, under-instructed and entirely subjective—could not stand up of itself."[21] *Susan Spray* (1931), one of her most successful novels, portrays a woman whose religious life, "under-instructed and entirely subjective," ends in tragedy. One can glimpse in her autobiographical *Three Ways Home* some of the extreme conflicts going on in the young girl whose ambitions led her to frustration—on the one hand through her parents' ideas on religion and on the other through the difficulty of getting her manuscript published.

But after seven months of waiting, Messrs. George Bell & Sons did publish *The Tramping Methodist.* It sold only eight hundred and fifty copies. The young author, called to the publisher's office, was not allowed to go unchaperoned. So, accompanied by her father, "beaming solemnly and never speaking unless spoken to," she received such kindness and encouragement that she felt "almost convinced that a brilliant career" was to be hers. At that moment, the last vestiges of religion gave place to the dazzlement of authorship.[22]

It might be well to note here that until Miss Kaye-Smith became a Roman Catholic, although religion appears in her works, it appears without conviction about any particular creed. She feels that this kept her from propagandizing. Actually, it results in a detachment, an objectivity which adds to her presentation of character and action. It is recognized, however, that through what Wayne Booth calls "the rhetoric of fiction,"[23] no author can escape writing his or her ideas and convictions. Throughout most of her early writing, Sheila Kaye-Smith appears to be groping for specific religious convictions. There is always, however, the preference for "High" rather than "Low" Church, but this seems to be more a matter of intuition and desire than intellectual choice.

The Tramping Methodist was "well printed, well bound and well advertised; it was also exceedingly well reviewed." The publicity emphasizes its author's youth, which accounts for the fact, in its author's opinion, that the "critics were therefore more ready to forgive . . . a plot that was a tangle of impossibilities and a view of life that was obviously second-hand and derived from other books." Some of them point out that she clearly knows nothing about Methodism, but had used her hero's preaching "to relate his wanderings through the countryside she loves."[24] Her response to this criticism is an example of the harshness with which she constantly judges her books: "most of them I think realized that my protagonist was really the country of the Rother Valley and my pilot a map of the Kent and Sussex borders. I was lucky to meet so much tolerance and understanding on my first appearance; for, sensitive as I had always been about my writing, I should have suffered badly from a harsh reception—and critics could be really harsh in those days of unsigned reviews."[25]

Even though the publisher's note to the New American Edition of *The Tramping Methodist* published in 1922, when Miss Kaye-Smith had attained popularity and fame, states that this "new edition . . . should prove of real and permanent value,"[26] the novel holds interest more as a promise of talent to be developed than as an artistic creation. It does, however, give "stark and extraordinarily vivid pictures of the spiritual deadness and degradation of England's national church and of the inhuman conditions of jails and criminal procedure in the early Nineteenth Century."[27] But these pictures lack the excellence of plot and characterization which a developing intelligence and artistic skill would supply to the later novels.

Starbrace (1909), her second novel, was written entirely from her imagination. This story of the desperate deeds of highwaymen depicts a life of incredible suffering. Miles Starbrace undergoes all kinds of pain, physical and emotional, and dies while scarcely more than a boy. He dies with apparent relief that his suffering is at last over. This soap opera of suffering went through at least nine American editions in 1926, at a time when its author's reputation was firmly established. At the time of its original publication, however, it sold even fewer copies than *The Tramping Methodist.*

Sheila Kaye-Smith calls her first two novels "the last of [her] schoolgirl outpourings." She adds that except for "their length and superior merit due to the fact that they had been carefully revised, there is very little difference between them and the contents of the penny exercise books."[28]

The violence in these two first novels shocked some of the readers, even though it is mild by today's standards. The fact that this violence came from the pen of a young woman added to the shock. The author recalls that at that time

girls were supposed to read—and presumably, if they ever wrote, to write—"books for girls." Methodist—either aped or the genuine expression of the adolescent boy-girl—to say nothing of the nature of the story, which contained a murder trial and lurid prison scenes, would be a severe shock to anyone expecting Pixie O'Shaughnessey. Some local readers, including the editor of the Hastings Newspaper, were charmingly appreciative, and some no doubt were excellently amused; but as far as certain others were concerned, I might just as well have called on my publisher without a chaperon.[29]

The appearance of this book in the local library astonished the people who knew its author "only as an awkward and silent girl with bookish tendencies and extraordinary clothes."[30]

III *Local Reputation*

Except for a few close friends, Miss Kaye-Smith kept herself aloof from the society of the town. She enjoyed being alone, as she was rather shy. She busied herself with lofty plans for the attainment of fame as a novelist. She admits that she took no interest in any politics later than the French Revolution, even though the suffragist movement was in full swing. But her neighbors took it for granted that, as she was a novelist, she must also be a suffragette. She recalls that "rumor knocked me down and blacked my eyes. I did not mind, for I was not opposed to Women's Suffrage—just not interested (I should think better of myself now if then I had at least done a little to help that nothing which should have been so much."[31]

Her reputation as suffragette, though undeserved, led her to be accused of burning down Levetleigh, the borough member's house, which was opposite her home, even though she slept all through the burning. The firemen testified that they had seen her at the window, "mocking the efforts of the fire-brigade and shouting 'Votes for Women'."[32] Her father had to expend great effort to clear her name at the police station, the fire brigade headquarters, and his club, where, she recalls, "scandal died last of all—if indeed it can be said to have died, for I believe that there are still people who think that I burned down Levetleigh. It is just the sort of thing a novelist would do."[33]

Her parents, although surprised, and not always agreeably, at their daughter's pouring forth of stories of rogues and vagabonds, stood by her loyally, offering little criticism. Nevertheless, Miss Kaye-Smith remembers a "sharply etched picture of [her] mother poised on the top bar of a stile and exclaiming passionately without context: 'Sheila, you're *not* to say, "I like 'em full-breasted." ' "[34]

Fortunately for the developing author, both parents took her literary career seriously, and when her literary agent suggested that she should see more of life, they even allowed her to stay alone at a ladies' club in London. This concession did not produce the anticipated result. But with the recognition, though slight, of her first two novels, she was enabled to give up writing her novels "on the dining-room table, with all the business, pleasure and strife of the family surging round"[35] and write them in a room of her own, although this room was in her parents' home.

IV   Reading

As well as being an avid writer, Miss Kaye-Smith was also an avid reader, devouring popular novels and classical writings with equal appetite. About the time of publication of her first two novels, she consciously attempted to go outside of conventional reading with the hope of formulating new beliefs. She "no longer wanted to be High Church." She "did not want to be an atheist," as she had had "enough of that at thirteen," but she "wanted desperately to be Progressive and Enlightened . . . free of Outworn Dogmas and Threadbare Conventions" and she "had the will to disbelieve."[36] Her readings at this time included Nietzsche, contrary renditions of biblical ideas by English divines, and Emanuel Swedenborg. It was Swedenborg whose ideas caused her to change the English governess in *Spell Land* (1910) into a Swedenborgian minister. She admits that she "did not succeed in keeping . . . religious enthusiasms out of *Spell Land* as she succeeded in keeping them out of later novels." She also admits that this novel is overloaded with ideas not her own.[37]

Nevertheless, she received an advance of forty pounds for *Spell Land*, ten pounds more than for *Starbrace*. This enabled her to take a trip to Paris. At this time she was "twenty-four in actual years, about nineteen in looks, and not more than sixteen in experience."[38] Although she still lived at home, she felt that she was definitely leading her own life, because she had friends who were unknown to her parents. Her parents remained unsuspicious and supportive.

Continuing to write, she published *Isle of Thorns* (1913) and *Three Against the World* (1914), both of which had poor sales. She rates *Isle of Thorns* as "silly" and *Three Against the World* as "forced and unreal," showing "an astonishing poverty of invention."[39] Her publishers may have agreed with this estimate in refusing her a contract for another book, but it is possible that the beginning of World War I, with its unsettling effect on British publishers, resulted in her loss of contract. Far more important writers than she, Arnold Bennett among them, were affected adversely at this time. At any rate, it was the first time she had been without a contract since *The Tramping Methodist*.

Before discussing her first really successful novel, *Sussex Gorse* (1916), it might be well to list those writers whom she calls her "masters." These include Samuel Richardson, Joseph Fielding, Lawrence Sterne, Tobias Smollett, Jane Austen, Emily Bronte, George Borrow, and William Blake. Although she calls Jane Austen her "Bible" and William Blake her "hymn book," she admits that they "have had no discernible influence on [her] style at all."[40] There may appear traces of the giants of English literature in her novels, particularly in the early ones, but after the first tentative efforts, as exemplified in the novels referred to above, her novels maintained a surety of technique and a depth of perception that could only stem from observation, conviction, skill—and talent. The first of these is *Sussex Gorse*.

CHAPTER 2

Impetus to Being: Convergence of Inner and Outer

BECAUSE Sheila Kaye-Smith's novels reflect the locale of Sussex, they have inevitably been linked with Thomas Hardy's. This, however, must be explained, as in many respects she is the opposite of Thomas Hardy. For example, her philosophy is very different, reflecting hope rather than pessimism. She does use Sussex as Thomas Hardy uses Wessex, as a backdrop against which characters move. In two novels which best call to mind the resemblance between the two authors, *Sussex Gorse* and Thomas Hardy's *The Return of the Native*, the use of the wasteland is different. Boarzell Moor appears almost as a character in *Sussex Gorse*, while Egdon Heath remains primarily a backdrop in *The Return of the Native*. In both authors, however, the atmosphere of place has its counterpart in the action, foretelling or amplifying the emotions of the characters.

I   Sussex Gorse

The hero of *Sussex Gorse*, Reuben Backfield, is obsessed with the single idea that he must purchase and develop several hundred acres of gorse-grown land, Boarzell Moor, which adjoins Odiam, the family farm. When his father dies, he becomes owner of Odiam and in a position to realize his ambition. He subjugates everyone in his life and attempts to force them to help him attain his dream. Reuben feels that only by being cruel and ruthless himself can he fight the cruelty and ruthlessness of Boarzell. His mother becomes the household drudge, while his brother Harry is sacrificed in a different way. While dynamiting tree roots, Reuben sets off a blast which blinds Harry and renders him a physical and mental cripple.

Harry's accident provides a wife for Reuben. Naomi, be-
trothed to Harry, turns to Reuben for love and comfort. She also,
according to Reuben, must be sacrificed for the taming of
Boarzell. He compels her to bear child after child, for Odiam
must have workers in order that money can be gained to buy
Boarzell. After bearing six sons and two daughters, Naomi's body
wears out, and she dies.

Still intent on his heart's desire, Reuben marries Rose, a young
woman thirty years his junior. He marries her for her comeliness,
her son-bearing ability, and the expectation of a dowry and an
inheritance. But even though Rose bears him two sons, she
refuses to be a household drudge. She also refuses to let Reuben
curb her flirtatious nature. He finally locks her out of the house
one night, and she runs off with her lover, Reuben's hired man.

As Reuben's sons grow to adulthood, they are forced by their
tyrannical father to work without wages. All but one, Pete, turn
against their father and escape the life he has planned for them
as part of his plan to subdue Boarzell. Albert, the eldest, runs off
to London and, after an unsuccessful career as writer, returns to
Odiam to die of consumption. Robert, twin of Pete, steals money
to run off with his sweetheart. He is caught and jailed. After
serving his term, he goes to Australia and sends for his still
faithful sweetheart. Pete, the only son who understands his
father's dream, works long and hard at the farm for many years.
However, when the dying Albert returns, his care of Albert leads
both him and Albert to religious conversion. When Albert dies,
Pete leaves Odiam to become an itinerant preacher.

Richard escapes through the friendly offices of the squire's
daughter who helps him to an education and a career as a
barrister in London. Later he marries her. Benjamin runs off to
sea and disappears. George, weak and epileptic, is forced by his
father to go outside to work on one of his "bad" days. He
strangles to death on the mud of Boarzell in an epileptic fit.

Of the two daughters, Tilly marries a neighboring farmer
whose land Reuben covets and finally attains. She leads a happy
and comfortable life until the failure of her husband's crops
brings the family to poverty. Reuben refuses to help, although he
offers to adopt her small son to make him heir to Odiam. Tilly,
horrified at the idea, chooses abject poverty rather than
surrender her son. The other daughter, Caro, love-starved and
humiliated all her life by the drudgery and unkindness she has

endured, finds a light love in a sailor. When he leaves her, she turns to prostitution.

Reuben feels he loves his two youngest sons, David and William, Rose's sons, as he has never loved any of his other children. However, they join the army and go off to war in South Africa. David is killed in action, and William decides to remain in South Africa.

Reuben has one chance at happiness. Alice Jury both understands and loves him. She is the only person who meets him as a human being. But she soon realizes that he is bound to Boarzell Moor. When he refuses to give up his plans for Boarzell, he loses his chance to make a life with her.

Reuben's story ends when he is eighty-five. He has no family and no friends, but he has Odiam. He has completely subdued Boarzell Moor, and he is content.

II   *Creation of Self*

Reuben Backfield creates himself as he creates arable land out of Boarzell Moor. The impetus to this creation is ambition. Even though the novel concerns itself with showing the effects of ambition on Reuben's considerable family, this is not the novel's major value. Many novels describe the effects of ambition, as indeed do *Macbeth* and *Oedipus the King*. Elizabeth Drew speaks of Reuben as "challenging God and man to prevent him accomplishing his quest—and finally triumphing."[1] But on its deepest level, the novel defines ambition, and the definition connects it with the creative forces with which one comes existentially into being. These creative forces may result in antihuman behavior, as they trample the human emotion of love in their wake. The effect of Reuben's ambition on his wives and family is not all negative, however, as his massive energy pounds them either into submission or into rebellion.

Naomi, Reuben's first wife, submits and dies performing her wifely act of providing sons to work Odiam. On the other hand, Rose, his second wife, escapes. The reader is led to believe that she becomes a fulfilled, happy woman, in love with a man more suited to her in age and disposition than Reuben. Albert's life becomes a wasteland of ineffectuality, as he lacks the financial help to start him on a creative career; yet through this waste, both he and Pete find salvation, and Pete escapes for a career of itinerant preaching. Robert, Richard, Benjamin, and Tilly all free themselves from their father's tyranny, and even though Caro's choice of freedom leads her to prostitution, she feels herself to be content.

The very harshness of the treatment becomes the impetus for escape. Reuben's failure to treat his family in a conventionally kind and considerate way allows them to break the bonds which might have, were he a more tolerant father, led them to accept a placid, unadventurous life as low paid farm laborers. And even though Reuben disowns them, thinks them mad for not sharing his ambition, he appears at times glad that he, alone, will fulfill his dream. If they cannot help, he feels, then let them get out and not hinder. Until he feels the stirrings of love for his last born, David and William, his emotions are not touched by their loss.

Reuben learns early that emotions hinder, rather than aid. To him the ordinary values of love, affection, devotion, and consideration present a stumbling block. From the moment he realizes that he "could fight this cruel tough thing only by being cruel and tough himself," he knows that he "must be ruthless as the wind that blustered over it, hard as the stones that covered it, wiry as the gorse roots that twisted in its marl."[2] He consciously stifles all tender emotions in order to prime himself for the nearly superhuman task he has determined to accomplish.

Critics of *Sussex Gorse* emphasize this aspect of the novel, and it is an important one. The plot builds on what happens in Reuben's struggle, showing the effect of this struggle on his family, as he slowly and tenaciously subdues Boarzell Moor. Robert Thurston Hopkins feels that "Sheila Kaye-Smith has admirably succeeded in describing the sullen, resolute, inflexible, countryman of the Weald in *Sussex Gorse*. There lives many a Reuben Backfield nowadays on the farms around Rye and Romney Marsh, returning slowly and sourly to his schemes, heedless of misfortune, death and the sweet and bitter love of women."[3] Hopkins' "nowadays" represents 1925, but one might counter that it is not only the Weald Country which harbors sullen, resolute, inflexible men (and women), that specimens are frequently seen today, in literature and in life.

Ordinarily, ambition has a negative connotation. To describe the effect of ambition on a person of ambition and on those surrounding him is to start out with the idea that ambition is evil and results in destruction of not only the person himself, but of others also. This, at least, is the view of Greek tragedy, but it is not necessarily Miss Kaye-Smith's view. As pointed out above, not all the effects of Reuben's ambition are negative, and whether one concludes that Reuben himself becomes the epitome of evil depends on one's point of view. To himself, he was a happy, fulfilled person, secure in a realized dream and unafraid to die.

Reuben's dream finds expression when he, at fifteen, attends Boarzell Fair, a yearly event. The novel opens with the conflict of opposing forces, Boarzell Moor and Boarzell Fair.

The Moor was on the eastern edge of the parish, five miles from Rye. Heaving suddenly swart out of the green watermeadows by Socknersh, it piled itself towards the sunrise, dipping to Leasan House. It was hummocked and tussocked with coarse grass. . . . In places the naked soil gaped in sores made by coney-warrens or uprooted bushes. Stones and roots, sharn, shards, and lumps of marl, mixed themselves into the wealden clay, which oozed in red streaks of potential fruitfulness through their sterility" (1).[4]

Boarzell Fair "had been held every year on Boarzell Moor for as long as the oldest in Peasmarsh could remember," but now on this October day in the year 1835, freehold rights are being challenged, and the local people can talk of nothing else. Reuben's father will surely lose the sixty acres he used to pasture his cows on. Reuben tells the farmer Ticehust that his father, mother, and brother Harry " 'doan't care, nuther—it's only me.' " Reuben knows that his father "still went whistling to the barn, because . . . he still had a bright fire, with a pretty wife and healthy boys beside it." And "Reuben's lip curled. He could not help despising his father for this ambitionless content" (5-6).

The opposing forces might be represented by Boarzell Moor,[5] wild, severe, uncontrolled, and uncontrollable, and Boarzell Fair, frivolous, civilized, and dedicated to the pursuit of pleasure. Reuben chooses Boarzell Moor, foregoing the pursuit of pleasure or even of the civilized virtues, and already at fifteen "his expression would have been kindly . . . were it not for a certain ruthlessness of the lips" (4).

Boarzell Moor itself is a paradox. The gorse is an "all-enveloping scent . . . a mysterious warm smell of peaches and apricots."[6] And there is

something in that scent which both mocked and delighted him. It was
an irony that the huge couchant beast of Boarzell should smell so sweet.
. . . But, after all, this subtle gorse-fragrance had its suitableness, for
though gorse may cast out the scent of soft fruit from its flowers, its
stalks are wire and its roots iron, its leaves are so many barbs for those
who would lay hands on its sweetness. It was like Boarzell itself, which
was Reuben's delight and his dread, his beloved and his enemy (108).

The attraction which Boarzell holds for Reuben cannot be
separated from the cruelty he feels it contains. It is a challenge
beyond human strength. And it is this challenge that he cannot
resist. He "churned the soil with his heel, and knew he could
conquer it. . . . He could plant those thistle-grounds with
wheat. . . . Coward! his father was a coward if he shrank from
fighting Boarzell. The land could be tamed just as young bulls
could be tamed. By craft, by strength, by toughness man could
fight the nature of a waste as well as of a beast. Give him
Boarzell, and he would have his spade in its red back, just as he
would have his ring in a bull's nose" (6). This need for proof of
selfhood, masked in a vow to tame the land, spurts from a depth
not completely explored by Sheila Kaye-Smith. But there are
hints. There is the fact that Reuben's parents prefer his brother
Harry to him. "Reuben looked at Harry with detachment. He
was not in the least jealous of his position as favorite son, he had
always accepted it as normal and inevitable. His parents did not
openly flaunt their preference . . . but one could not help
seeing that their attitude towards the elder boy was very
different from what they felt for the younger" (18). Harry is a
beautiful boy, of a loving and dependent nature, "whereas
Reuben seemed equally indifferent to caresses or commands. He
was not a bad son, but he never appeared to want affection, and
was always immersed in dark affairs of his own" (18).

Even though it is not pointed out, the hint is there. Reuben,
subconsciously aware that he lacks what his parents obviously
find charming in Harry, perhaps consciously rejects those
qualities he does not have and cultivates the discipline of
hardness, ruthlessness, and power to take their place. In
accepting a challenge too great for anyone else, the taming of
Boarzell, he can prove to himself that he is great—greater, even,
than anyone else. "Surely in all Sussex, in all England, there had
never been such an undertaking as this . . . and when he was
triumphant, had achieved his great ambition, won his heart's

desire, how proud, how glorious he would be among his children" (107–108).

But whatever his motivation for the conquest of Boarzell Moor, it becomes intimately connected with his being. He carries on a love-hate relationship with it, for Boarzell represents part of him. He is Boarzell. When he battles with those who are pulling down the enclosures which will remove Boarzell from the common land, "he had one last visit of that furious hate which had made him join the battle—hate of those who had robbed his father of Boarzell, and hate of Boarzell itself, because he would never be able to tame it as one tames a bull with a ring in its nose" (12). As he receives a flogging, swift punishment for his part in the melee,

that hatred which had run through him like a knife just before he lost consciousness in the battle of Boarzell, suddenly revived and stabbed him again. It was no longer without focus, and it was no longer without purpose. . . . He was suffering for Boarzell . . . he, Reuben, had been robbed—and he had fought for Boarzell, and now he was bearing shame and pain for Boarzell. Somehow he had never till this day, till this moment, been so irrevocably bound to the land he had played on as a child, on which he had driven his father's cattle. . . . Boarzell was his, and at the same time he hated Boarzell. For some strange reason he hated it as much as those who had taken it from him and as those who were punishing him because of it. He wanted to tame it, as a man tames a bull, with a ring in its nose. (16)

It is then and there that he swears he will "tame and conquer Boarzell," for the "rage, the fight, the degradation, the hatred of the last twelve hours should not be in vain." He will make all of Boarzell his, not only the part stolen from his father, but even its "mocking, nodding crest of fire." He will "subdue" it, make it "bear grain as meekly as the most fruitful field," make it "feed fat cattle." Then it will "make the name of Odiam great, the greatest in Sussex. It should be his, and the world should wonder." He leaves the whipping post "with a great oath in his heart, and a thin trickle of blood on his chin" (16).

In these feelings stirring the heart of fifteen year old Reuben lies the motivation for the sacrifices of self and family that come in the wake of the "great oath." Reuben has transferred his low self-esteem to the dream of the glory that will be his when he shall have accomplished what seems to be humanly impossible.

And it remains "humanly impossible," as in its accomplishment, Reuben gives up his humanity. Thus Boarzell Moor takes on the aspect of a character in the novel, as Reuben makes his vow to subdue it.

Sheila Kaye-Smith's presentation of the land as having human characteristics, as being a force, like a person, to be subdued, goes beyond the presentation of other writers who wrote about the land of Sussex, notably Thomas Hardy and Rudyard Kipling. Thomas Hardy and Rudyard Kipling used the locale of Sussex for background, for mood, and for unchanging reality. In *Sussex Gorse* Sheila Kaye-Smith makes the land of Sussex the antagonist in Reuben's battle for life.

Malcolm Cowley finds that the "earth of Sussex might be called the chief of her dramatic personae." He believes that "nowhere does she call this character into being more forcibly than in *Sussex Gorse*."[7] Also, Robert Thurston Hopkins points out that there is a close parallel between Boarzell Moor and Reuben's actions. "There is a wonderful haunting power about Sheila Kaye-Smith's word pictures of Boarzell Common. She uses the place spirit as a medium at times transfiguring, at times interpretive, at times heavy with doom, and this facile use of environment as a barometer which forecasts sunshine and tempest in her story has never been used with such magic since Thomas Hardy gave us those mysterious pictures of Bere Heath in *Tess of the D'Urbervilles*."[8] Thus, the characteristics of Boarzell find their counterpart in Reuben, for the moor "became the very core of temptation to Reuben, lulling his soul into a kind of secret passion" (134–35).

It becomes imperative to note the extremely close relationship of Reuben to Boarzell Moor, as Reuben's actions find both their being, and their reason for being, in his alliance with, as well as his conflict with, Boarzell.

The blunting of human sensibilities of consideration and kindness finds its excuse in the necessity of cruelty. As he takes over Odiam, Reuben orders that all small comforts of family living be sacrificed to an economy which will permit the hoarding of money for the purchase of more land. Reuben never examines his major premise—that Boarzell must be conquered— because to do so would be to question his own right to be, to become. He struggles for Boarzell because he substitutes it for himself. He personalizes it. He rationalizes his callousness, because he "had set himself to build a house, and for the sake of that house there was nothing, whether of his own or of others, that he could not tame, break down, and destroy" (36). It is the perfect sanction for a deep selfishness.

Reuben can, also, find solace in Boarzell to slake the feelings of jealousy which rise when he sees the tender, loving relationship of his brother Harry and Naomi. He "had a love more beautiful than Harry's whose comeliness would stay unwithered through the years, whose fruitfulness would make him great, whose allure was salted with a hundred dangers." The reek of the earth rising to his nostrils is "the scent of his love." As he moves his hand over the short grass, he is "caressing" it. And finally, as he embraces Boarzell "with wideflung trembling arms," he can cry, "'My Land!—mine!—Mine!'" (40). As he accepts the substitute of Boarzell for a loving human being, he allows all the repressed power, cruelty, and drive of his innermost being to vent itself on Boarzell, blaming on Boarzell his actions to others on behalf of Boarzell. It is his rationalization for his complete withdrawal from the community of humans.

The love-hate relationship he feels with Boarzell (and himself) brings fear as he realizes the uncanny presence of Boarzell. When Harry's blood is spilled in the dynamite accident, Reuben feels that Boarzell is "drinking . . . eagerly, greedily" the blood, and he has a "vague, a sudden, a ridiculous fear . . . for the first time he felt afraid of the thing he had set out to conquer—for the first time Boarzell was not just unfruitful soil, harsh heather clumps and gorse-roots—it was something personal, opposing, vindictive, blood-drinking" (47).

His consideration of Boarzell as a bloodthirsty entity gives Reuben an excuse for disclaiming responsibility for Harry's accident. He begins to think that if Harry died, he, Reuben, would have killed him because he "had ignored his own inexperience and played splashy tricks with his new land." Again he rationalizes. "But no—he had not killed him—it was Boarzell, claiming a victim in the signal-rite of subjection" (47). Reuben, in renouncing responsibility for his actions, begins on the downward path which leads to inhumanity.

In transferring to Boarzell the havoc he wreaks on his brother, and later on his mother, his wives, and his children, Reuben can divorce himself from the burden of responsibility for his actions. His alliance with Boarzell helps him to shun the burden. When he is outdoors, the "heaviness, the vague remorse over Harry's accident grows lighter." And "out on Boarzell, which was the cause of his trouble, they grew lightest of all" (50).

Added to the shirking of responsibility for his actions is his desire to get away from the limiting effect of being human. Out on Boarzell, he experiences

a wider life, a life which took no reck of sickness or horror or self-reproach. The wind which stung his face and roughed his hair, the sun which tanned his nape as he bent to his work, the smell of the earth after rain, the mists that brewed in the hollows at dusk, and at dawn slunk like spirits up to the clouds . . . they were all part of something too great to take account of human pain—so much greater than he that in it he could forget his trouble, and find ease and hope and purpose— even though he was fighting it. (50)

The attraction compels him, even while he realizes its menace. The exhilaration of the fight for selfhood, paradoxically, destroys that selfhood by giving it a cause to shun responsibility for its actions.

Reuben, if divorced from moral considerations, is splendid in his strength and purpose. His mother enjoys being part of that strength, even though it means a life of drudgery for her. Naomi also enjoys Reuben's strength, as she remembers "the swing of his arm, the crash of the axe on the trunk, the bending of his back as he pulled it out, the muscles swelled under the skin . . . and then the tingling creep in her own heart, that sudden suffocating thrill which had come to her there beside Harry in the gloam. . . . the intoxication of the weak by the strong" (64).

Thus Reuben's attraction binds Naomi, even though she runs out of the marriage chamber decorated with dead flowers by the crazed Harry "panting and sobbing with rage," to meet something "even blacker than darkness." And although the "rage was stifled from her lips with kisses," (76-77) her surrender to the attractive power of Reuben finally leads to her death, a death she finds preferable to life with him.

Naomi comes to recognize Reuben's likeness to Boarzell, for "sometimes she found herself thinking of him not so much as a man as a thing; she saw in him no longer the loving if tyrannical husband, but a law, a force, to which she and everyone else must bow. She even notices a kind of likeness between him and

Boarzell—swart, strong, cruel, full of an irrepressible life" (88). This likeness to Boarzell becomes physical, as his skin becomes "the colour of the soil he tilled" while his teeth were "big, white, and pointed, like an animal's" (101).

As he delivers himself, body, heart, and soul to Boarzell, it stirs him as another man would be stirred by love:

Today he inspected his crop, and planned for its reaping. With parted lips and a faint sensuous gleam in his eyes he watched it bow and ripple before the little breeze. . . . He drank in the scent of the baking awns, the heat of the sun-cracked earth. It was all dear to him—all ecstasy. And he was dear to himself because the beauty of it fell upon him . . . . Oh Lord! it was good to be a man, to feel the sap of life and conquest running in you, to be battling with mighty forces, to be able to fight seasons, elements, earth, and nature. (112)

It is not surprising that, connected to Boarzell with the innermost part of himself, he hardly mourns Naomi's death, even though he realizes that he has killed her by forcing her to an excess of childbearing. He is sorry, but "if he had it all to do over again he would do it, for the sake of the land which was so much more to him than her life" (117). He comes, then, to feel that it is "this hateful land which had killed her" (118). Gradually he rationalizes away all responsibility as "the lust for conquest drove away regret. He had no more cause for self-reproach than an officer who loses a good soldier in battle" (121). At this point he needs no one, accepts responsibility for no one, for "Boarzell was always there to be loved and fought for, even if he had no heart or arm but his own" (190).

Reuben can sustain the idea that his dream takes precedence over the wishes of others until he meets Alicy Jury, for Alice Jury is the first person who meets him as an equal. In her love for him, and his for her, she recognizes the force that drives him, and she attempts to convince him, without success, that the force will destroy him. But she cannot persuade him to accept her love and leave unattained his plans for Boarzell, for Boarzell is himself. "In challenging Boarzell he had challenged the secret forces of his own body, all the riot of hope and weakness and desire that go to make a man. The battle was not to be won except over the heaped bodies of the slain, and on the summit of the heap would lie his own" (266). So, because Boarzell is "his love as well as his

enemy—more, far more to him than Alice," he gives up this
chance for normal happiness, convinced that "the last enemy to
be destroyed is Love" (330).

In destroying this last "enemy," Reuben effectively closes off
the slight connection that still remains between him and his
fellow humans. In accepting only his own values, he puts himself
apart. He is disliked "not because anyone particularly envied him
the land he bought so eagerly and so generously shaped, but
because of his utter disregard of what other men prized and his
willingness to sacrifice it for the sake of what they did not prize
at all" (396).

Alice Jury recognizes this in refusing to accept him as long as
he carries on his ambition for Boarzell. She feels that "we can't
forgive each other—for being happy in different ways" (447).
She recognizes, here, the necessity of a definition of self through
the definition assigned by others. But Reuben needs no such
definition. In his climb to freedom from all human ties—even the
greatest, love—he finds that the "earth for which he had
sacrificed all, was enough for him now that all else was gone"
(456). He makes his choice in freedom, knowing that what other
men prize he must sacrifice. He would have liked to have had
both worlds. Knowing he cannot, he chooses Boarzell.

And the choice satisfies him. Although he never gains wisdom,
never learns compassion, never participates in community, his
eyes are "full of that benign serenity which one so often sees in
the eyes of old men—just as if he had not ridden roughshod over
all the sweet and gentle things of life" (457).

Accomplishing his goal, he is happy, for "the wind, the rain,
dawns, dusks and darkness were all given to him as the crown of
his faithfulness. He had bruised Nature's head—and she had
bruised his heel, and given him the earth as his reward" (462).
Thus, as the story ends, and Reuben at the age of eighty-five
contemplates his life, he can tell himself, " 'I've won and it's bin
worthwhile. . . . I've lived to see my heart's desire. I've fought
and I've suffered, and I've gone hard and gone rough and gone
empty—but I haven't gone in vain. It's all bin worth it. Odiam's
great and Boarzell's mine—and when I die . . . well, I've lived so
close to the earth all my days that I reckon I shan't be afraid to
lie in it at last' " (462).

Thus through his great love affair with Boarzell Moor, Reuben has come into his full being. He has not learned wisdom through suffering; he has not come to despair through rejection. He has come to elation, knowing that he has accomplished his life's work. The rejection by family, by friends, by the woman he loves, means little or nothing to him. The material rewards of his sacrifices mean nothing. In the striving, the sacrificing, the conquering, he has found his manhood, his being; paradoxically, in this striving, sacrificing, and conquering he has thrown away all that would have made this being human, if one takes as a definition of humanity the ability to love.

Reuben stands alone at the end, a monster of strength, a monster of power, a monster of satisfaction, secure in his monstrous egocentricity. But he has his rationalization. In rejecting the community of human beings, in forcing his family to his will, where possible, or rejecting them when it is not, he can claim that the responsibility is Boarzell's.

In presenting Reuben Backfield, Sheila Kaye-Smith presents the powerful idea that ambition can be a creative as well as a destructive force. Unfortunately for her art, the idea takes over. Except for Reuben, and in a lesser way Naomi and Alice, characters are primarily props to impede or advance Reuben's actions. The point of view, of course, is primarily Reuben's, but as Reuben's actions all revolve around Boarzell and his relation to it, actions and images become repetitious. The author simply explains too much.

But beyond these defects, defects which might be readily excused when one realizes the youth of their author, there remains a curious and somber study of the dark side of human nature free of the softening effects of civilized virtues. Reuben rules Odiam and subjugates Boarzell. Odiam suggests "odium"—hate, contempt, anger—all part of Reuben's nature. This inner hatred, contempt, and anger are necessary if Boarzell (which suggests a boar—a savage, uncastrated, wild pig) is to be subdued. The animal imagery sets the basis of the struggle. Animal must subdue animal. The action of wrestling with animal nature (represented by Boarzell) forces Reuben into utter disregard for human life, even though that life is presumably dear to him.

Unbridled emotion (in this case gnawing ambition), then, cuts through the veneer of the civilizing virtues which are based on concern for others, and results, not only in lack of concern, but in women bred to death or exhaustion, weak men blinded, mothers reduced to slavery. Complete disregard of other human beings and their needs is the price of realization of Reuben's need, exactly as it was the price of Adolph Hitler's. Sheila Kaye-Smith presents in *Sussex Gorse,* the one-sided, egotistical monster. Yet Reuben, subjectively, feels himself content. Outside of the ethical or moral vision, the author appears to be saying, there is only oneself. No one else counts. It is perhaps surprising, but artistically valid, that Sheila Kaye-Smith allows Reuben his contentment.

Comparisons between Reuben and Heathcliff of *Wuthering Heights* or Rochester of *Jane Eyre* seem to be inevitable. All three characters reveal dark, somber natures, driven by a mysterious maniacal force. Yet the comparison ends when one considers the impetus to action and the outcome of action relevant to the three. Reuben has only his inner compulsion, which revolves inward. Heathcliff has his alter ego, his complement, Catherine, without whom he is only partly human. Rochester, of course, is redeemed from his suffering ego through the love of a good woman. Reuben remains, then, the embodiment of an inward drive for mastery, in his case of nature, just as Adolph Hitler remains the embodiment of a like inward drive for mastery, in his case of the world.[9] Both cause destruction, even though the scale is different. Undoubtedly Adolph Hitler would have, like Reuben, considered his life, despite the holocaust he caused, worthwhile.

There is in *Sussex Gorse* that particular insight which comes through art, a special something seen beyond the lines of the characters. It appears in Reuben's creative drive, his necessity for putting himself on the line, for consciously choosing a task ordinarily seen as humanly impossible. Even though unfortunate for his children and the women who loved him, it is fortunate for him. He achieves the creation of himself. As a study of the effects of a gross ambition, *Sussex Gorse* compels interest. As a psychological insight into the connection between ambition and the power of an individual to create himself through a terrible drive, *Sussex Gorse* goes further. It gives insight into the motivation of the achievers of the world (monstrous though some of their achievements turn out to be), and in some way, it draws all humans into its circle.

III   Tamarisk Town

Another novel which explores ambition, *Tamarisk Town* (1919), presents a protagonist whose ambition brings him not to his "heart's desire" but to his destruction. In *Tamarisk Town* Sheila Kaye-Smith develops and enlarges the theme of ambition, connecting it to the creative force of love.

Like Reuben Backfield, Edward Monypenny, the protagonist of *Tamarisk Town*, grows through a consuming ambition, but unlike Reuben, he turns on his ambition and destroys that for which he has given his life. The story begins in the year 1857. Edward Monypenny, a man of twenty-eight, young in years and experience but old in actions, finds himself able at last to realize his dream of making the town in which he lives, Marlingate (Tamarisk Town), a seaside resort which will surpass Brighton in beauty and elegance. He has inherited a thousand acres of land from his mother. He has always participated in the municipal concerns of the town as an alderman, but now he has the money to actively pursue his dream. He interests a London businessman, Becket, in financing his scheme, and he engages a young, brilliant architect, Decimus Figg, to plan his vision. With the help of these two, one supplying the money and the other supplying the blueprint, Monypenny, using his own strong personality, persuades the other members of the board of aldermen to accede to his plans.

The town grows and thrives under the careful planning of Monypenny. Becket, interested in the town beyond the normal interest of a financial backer, comes for a season to Marlingate, bringing along Morgan Wells, the young governess of his four motherless children. Monypenny, although attracted to Morgan, realizes that she falls below his social standing and would never be accepted by the Marlingate society in which he moves. Morgan, however, falls in love with him. In her desire to make herself Monypenny's social equal, she marries Becket. Through this action and through her careful education of herself into the ways of the wealthy, she becomes Monypenny's social equal.

When Morgan returns to Marlingate as Mrs. Becket, Monypenny realizes not only that she is equal to him socially, but that she exerts a curious power to draw him to her. Calling her an "enchantress," he finally succumbs to her considerable charms and finds himself partner with her in an illicit love affair, an affair reminiscent of that of the mayor in Thomas Hardy's *The Mayor of Casterbridge*. Torn between his love for Morgan le Fay, as he calls her, and his respectability as the mayor of Marlingate, he chooses to give Morgan up rather than to run away with her and give up the town he idolizes. Morgan, after she has experienced on a stolen holiday what love really could be like with Monypenny, realizes that she can never go back to their secret love. She throws herself over a cliff in order to end her misery and to give Monypenny back to his town.

After her suicide, Monypenny realizes that Morgan had given him life and that he will be a mere shell without her. Blaming the town for her death, he vows to avenge her by destroying what he had so painstakenly built up over many years. Also, in his loneliness he marries Fanny Vidler, the niece of one of the town's aldermen, a man who is his friend. Fanny loves him, but he does not love her, and although they have a son, Ted, Monypenny gradually withdraws from Fanny, leaving a lack in her life.

As Ted grows to manhood, he sees the growing destruction of Marlingate and wishes to stem it. He is like his father once was in his dream for Marlingate. To this end, he opposes his father at town meetings. Finally, Monypenny tells Ted that he, Monypenny, is deliberately destroying the town, although he does not tell Ted why. Ted believes that his father is losing his mind.

Ted marries Lindsay, the daughter of Morgan and Becket, against his father's wishes. Monypenny sees a danger to Ted in Ted's desire to restore Marlingate, as he still believes that Marlingate has destroyed his happiness. He persuades Lindsay to encourage Ted to emigrate to America, where his considerable architectural skill might be used in the building of Los Angeles. An added benefit will be that Ted will no longer be able to interfere with Monypenny's almost completed destruction of Marlingate.

Finally, aged before his time and ill with heart trouble, Monypenny dies as a result of a rock thrown by one of the rowdy crowd allowed into Marlingate by Monypenny's encouragement of the town's destruction. The rock hits him as he stands on a balcony reading the riot act to the crowd during a riot.

In an epilogue, Ted comes back to Marlingate to participate in the unveiling of a statue to his father. Ted realizes that the town is now a third rate resort. In fact, the crowd milling around shows more interest in the carnival atmosphere than in the memory of his father. When the crowd disperses, only the sightless statue of Monypenny stares out to sea.

IV Creation and Destruction of Self

Like *Sussex Gorse*, which opens with a description of Boarzell Moor, *Tamarisk Town* opens with a description of Marlingate, the town which, like the moor in *Sussex Gorse*, becomes a living entity. The town is "a tumble of blacks and reds, a mass of broken colours flung between the hills, into the little scoop between the woods and the sea. It lay there like a thing flung down, heaped and broken, rolling to the very edge of the waves, and held from falling into them only by its thick, battered Town Wall."[10] Like Boarzell Moor in *Sussex Gorse*, Marlingate, or Tamarisk Town (the names are used interchangeably in the novel), assumes the status of a character. Also, like Boarzell for Reuben Backfield, Marlingate becomes the convenient scapegoat for Monypenny's actions. The town symbolizes a beautiful woman, for "those wise in other ways than the weather's saw in the town a queer, changeling beauty, as if it lay between the hills a fairy's town" (1). Monypenny is attracted to the town as he would be to a beautiful woman, but as he makes the town (and eventually destroys it), he makes and destroys himself. The town, therefore, symbolizes both something outside and something inside himself.

As Reuben Backfield in *Sussex Gorse* is the moor, so Monypenny is the town. Sometimes "it seemed almost as if the woods and the sea would soon fly together in some strange embrace, crushing the town between them, swallowing up all his dreams for Marlingate in that one great dream wherein he and Marlingate swam together like bubbles, pledged to a divine destruction" (2). To Monypenny, Marlingate seems "a little bit of time poised between two huge, threatening eternities," and he "would feel himself upholding the town with his manhood" (2). Like Backfield, Monypenny attempts to transcend his limitations as a human being, pitting himself not against a moor, but against the woods and sea.

Also, the town represents the civilized, the genteel, the socially acceptable side of Monypenny, for Monypenny is a snob.

But there is more than status involved in his plans to make Marlingate a "paradise" for the genteel. Neither the genteel nor this paradise he will create count as much as "the labours that should raise it" (7). Thus the doing represents the achievement. Monypenny, in raising the town to his own standards of beauty and gentility, will consciously bring into being that side of him that will conquer the still unrecognized wild side of him. Open country has for him a "repulsion and a charm." It is "the life outside his life" which he both loves and fears. The woods are like "a wild animal crouching at his door" (8).

These subconscious forces (in Greek terms the Apollonian and the Dionysian, in psychological terms the ego and the id) form the conflict in Monypenny. He puts these conflicting desires into symbols of the town and the sea and the woods. It seems to him "as if the wind linked up the woods and the sea—it joined their sighings, it mixed their savours, it seemed to proclaim the alliance of these two against his town" (23).

As he forms his ambition, Monypenny's dream for Marlingate removes it from his conscious brain as desire for power, and into an abstraction where, like Backfield, he wishes to transcend the boundary of his own limitations as a human being. "His dreams were at once the fruit and forcing-bed of his activities. . . . The whole thing would glow and glitter and triumph in Monypenny's brain, with behind it all a strange aching sense of the unsatisfied, of inadequacy even in fulfilment of a reaching out beyond hope and desire" (22). His egocentricity convinces him that Marlingate belongs to him. He represents the "vital spark of a business that without him was only trifling and sordid—he was the spirit of that to which the others provided a clumsy, rather unclean body" (29). The other members of the municipal governing board regard Marlingate primarily as a business venture, although some members come to share some of Monypenny's aesthetic pleasure in it. Some of them, indeed, led to this aesthetic beauty by Monypenny, oppose him strongly when finally he destroys the town. But like a benevolent despot, Monypenny regards the people who come to Marlingate as "his children, whose gambols were due to his indulgence, who owed him their delight, even their being." So he "beamed on them, and blessed them in his heart" (37).

As he builds up and blesses his town, Monypenny's repressed

side fears the woods, even though he owns them. He feels that the woods do not belong to him, even though he gives the orders for their destruction. He feels "vaguely uncomfortable, almost superstitious," as if he knows that "no good would come of meddling with these woods" (43). For the woods represent a part of himself which he represses, as "the wood seemed to be trying to draw him into its secret life." He is disturbed, for he imagines that from somewhere in the woods "life might suddenly take shape, half human, half animal—half loving, half alien" (4). And life does take shape from the woods, for as his heart suddenly twists in fear, he sees two great dark eyes staring at him, and he sees these eyes as "the eyes of some creature, half animal, half human, a fawn, a fairy" and as they look they seem "to call" (44). The eyes belong to Morgan.

This fear-love relationship with Morgan gives the impetus to his actions in loving and leaving Morgan, but it also represents his subconscious. Morgan both troubles and entices him, for to him she is an enchantress. Convincing himself of her power over him, he refuses to acknowledge the buried passions he represses.

Morgan, secure at this point in her love for Monypenny, enjoys being his enchantress. She tells her young charges about an enchantress called Morgan le Fay "who could . . . turn towns into woods and castles into mushrooms and people into seashore pebbles, and at last was able to bewitch the great king himself, so that he gave her his magic sword" (60). Like her namesake, Morgan accepts her lover's magic sword (his control over his passions). But Monypenny reneges and, grasping control once more, fails to see that it is in the reneging, rather than in the relinquishing of control, that his destruction comes.

The love affair between Morgan and Monypenny comes into being through conscious effort on her part and through basic, although unrecognized, needs on his part. Morgan is a free spirit, a woman untrammeled by conventional standards, primitive, seductive, and daring. She desires him with the "passion of a creature inexperienced, unawakened, and at the same time merciless to itself and others in its cravings, proud with the reckless pride that only the half-civilized can know" (66).

As well as being recipient of Monypenny's passion, Morgan also represents this passion. She is the primitive side of Monypenny, which opposes the civilized side. All of Monypenny's dreams for his town find a basis in civilization: the woods that must be destroyed to make place for buildings; the American Ground, home of the outcasts of the town, which must be replaced by a park; the townspeople who must exist to serve only the socially prominent. Finding passionate fulfillment with Morgan means relinquishing the dreams for the town (his civilized side).

Although on one level Monypenny's ambition lies intrinsically entwined with the rise in prominence of his town, he realizes that his dreams outpace his ability to realize them. He grows used to a "sense of 'beyondness' which seemed to attaint his ideals for the town" (67). This restlessness, this searching for something beyond, this attempt to overcome his human limitations accounts for his fall when faced with the sexual delights offered by Morgan. He blames her spell as her eyes seem to be "drawing him into their depths, sucking him down into themselves like two treacherous whirlpools of untroubled surface and devouring heart" (70).

But, as he feels the pull toward the passionate, the uncontrolled, the Dionysian side of his nature, he runs to safety into the municipal affairs of Marlingate "like a hunted animal burrowing into the earth for safety." Under Marlingate's "comfortable, solid bricks," he will "bury this new disquiet" (71). Again he blames Morgan, for he is the "hunted animal." Yet, he is ambivalent, for at the picnic she arranges, he wishes he were among the gorse-clumps to "roll on the thyme" (79).

When he succumbs to her charms in a passionate embrace, he knows that she represents danger because she is "a woman of the woods." He equates her with the woods around Marlingate and finds "something prophetic in his shrinking" from them, in his sense that the woods are like a "hungry beast prowling round his town" (81).

Yet his feelings are paradoxical. He senses the danger to his innermost being in succumbing to her invitation, while at the same time, he experiences "something exalted, something much more than either he or she, almost as if he had overtaken and seized at last that flitting dream which had always run ahead of his desires" (95). The ecstasy which Backfield experiences in his contemplation of Boarzell (in *Sussex Gorse*), Monypenny experiences in his intimacy with Morgan. Both men attempt to extend their human limitation, literally to get outside of themselves:

Backfield through his love affair with his moor; Monypenny through his love affair with his town, but in addition, through his love affair with Morgan, who challenges his town. Morgan's pull is stronger and more satisfactory, for Monypenny has a "sense of possessing all things . . . of having reached out at last beyond the illusion of his desires and grasped that reality for which he had unconsciously striven" (87).

With Morgan as the liberating force, the means through which he can free his repressed part, Monypenny can experience that heightened awareness which the full use of his powers brings.[11] But he cannot thus easily achieve his growth toward the deepest impulses of his being. He has for too long chanelled his energies toward the seeking of ego satisfaction in status. Still the snob, still the statusseeker, he rejects these authentic impulses which draw him to Morgan and chooses his town. He pities "this poor little thing who sought to measure herself against his town" (92), and he wonders "how he ever could have risked his dear safety and freedom, the prop and span of his endeavor" (95). Safe from the liberating influence of Morgan and free to accept the confining bonds of conventionality, he vows that he will never again "let a woman snare him. He might see the reality and wisdom of love for those who had no other calling, but he had consecrated himself to more enduring things, and he would never forget how for one moment love had made him stagger before his ambition, risk its glories for the magic of a girl's eyes and lips, and unsubstantial things of wind and sea" (95).

Monypenny fails to realize that the "more enduring things" for which he sacrifices Morgan are the very things which come into being when he acts selfishly. He finally sacrifices these "enduring things" because what would have really endured — Morgan's love for him and his for her — has been forever lost through his sacrifice of her to these "enduring things." His creativity becomes tarnished with egocentricity.

Monypenny's creative powers reveal themselves in the creation of Marlingate as a watering place which should be the most beautiful watering place ever built. In creating Marlingate, therefore, he creates himself as the creator of beauty as well as the benevolent despot who dispenses this beauty to the worthy, but only to the worthy.

His aesthetic endeavors for Marlingate base themselves on his egocentric desire for power. Because he is unable to risk himself in the complete giving of himself in love to Morgan, he needs the power over others to secure his own ego: "it gave him a proud thrill . . . to think that it was his brain and effort which had made the town what it was, not only through their own direct achievement, but through the glorious indirectness of their dominion over others—so that he was in fact as well as in spirit the builder of Marlingate, a Briareus fifty-headed and hundred-armed" (102–103). Thus he aligns himself with the Olympic deities against the lawlessness of the Titans, peace and order overcoming the wild and disorderly forces of nature.

Refusing to recognize his needs or his part in attempting to fulfill them, Monypenny realizes that it was another Monypenny who had once been mad, "a changeling who by some spell had been freakishly set in his place for a few wild moments . . . but now merely haunted the woods which day by day Marlingate drove further from its streets" (104). As he blames enchantment for the actions he dare not recognize as his own, he forces, by domesticating the woods, a victory for the Olympic deities against the Titans.

The creativity which finds its being in Monypenny's creation of Marlingate substitutes for the creativity he could call into being were he not afraid of relaxing his control. Decimus Figg, the creative architect of Marlingate and as close a friend as Monypenny ever makes, attempts to make Monypenny realize that Marlingate will never satisfy his creative impulses. Figg feels that Monypenny was born to be an artist or a lover, for "love is the artistic culmination of desire, just as poetry is the artistic culmination of speech—and real love is about as rare as real poetry" (108–109). But Monypenny disagrees and answers, " 'My dear Figg, I was born to be Mayor of Marlingate' " (109).

When he becomes mayor of Marlingate by popular acclaim, he sees himself in royal terms. His "throne was built and he ascended it" (112). Like a king, he tastes his power, not only over the town, but also over himself, for in building Marlingate, he has built himself. "At thirty-five he had won his great ambition, still young and full of work he had seen the effort of his life materialize. Marlingate was what he had planned to make it, and he was Mayor of Marlingate" (112–13). But even more important is

this battle he had won over circumstances, himself, that weakening
sense of "beyondness," that unrest of the woods and the sea. . . . The
woods were now being cut and clipped into the order of the Town Park,
the sea was shut away beyond the shining austerity of the Marine
Parade. His little bit of time had been able to subdue those two
boasting forces of eternity, and he himself, who had found their
treacheries within him, wore a chain, the Mayor's chain of office—the
heavy pompous yoke that bound him forever to the triumph he had
won. (113)

Even as he glories in the accomplishment of his dream, he
recognizes that the dream carries with it a "yoke." When Morgan
returns to Marlingate, he is "by some inexplicable means relieved
of his Mayoral chain" (118). Morgan represents freedom for him,
the part of himself which would liberate his creativity, his love,
his humanity. But he is relieved to see that she, as Becket's wife,
"had not learned for nothing the wisdom of towns," and he has no
fear that she will try to "bring him back into that terrible place
which his soul dreaded between the woods and the sea"
(119-20).

Yet she does bring him back, to an adulterous affair this time,
but he has already learned "for the first time that his town was
built of dreams and shadows, cobwebs of desire, and little
rustling winds of regret" (124). Symbolically, his attempt to gain
his own immortality through his creation of his town has ended in
the realization that his attempt has been based on unreality.

Feeling himself drawn to the fishing smacks getting ready to
put out to sea, he finds the reality of Marlingate in the life of the
common fishermen. He finds himself "wanting to share that life
which was so characteristic of Marlingate and yet so remote from
its present activities, which had been of old time, and perhaps
would still be when all the rest had departed" (125-26).

Once again the earthy, the necessary, the humble activities
shared by all humans call to his repressed emotions. He has
always scorned the humble workers, but now he accepts their
invitation to join them in the morning's catch. Left to himself on
the fishing boat, he muses about his town and his life. "His little
refuge between the woods and the sea had betrayed him—his bit
of time had crumbled—but its eternal boundary remained, the
great whole of which Marlingate was a part, and to which its
ghost, so restless and troubling tonight belonged, the deep from

which it was taken to which it would return" (125). From his vantage point on the boat, Marlingate becomes unreal. "He watched its man-coloured brightness as a man might watch a bubble, and as he watched more and more of a bubble it became to him—a glowing iridescent dream, unreal, transient, mere air and water, bright with mock colours which were only the reflections of the eternal things around it" (128).

Marlingate, which had been the be-all and the end-all of his existence, now takes its place in his dreamlike thoughts as a mere drop in time and eternity. The time and eternity he had attempted to conquer through his creation of Marlingate are, in effect, unconquerable. In his dream, that night, he feels "shut up in Marlingate, he could not breathe, he was choking, panting, struggling," but when he wakes, he knows that he is "secure in the midst of his solemn, ordered existence, no prisoner in Dead-Man's Town, but Mayor of Marlingate" (130).

Although he now recognizes that forces are pulling him in opposite directions, his unrest needs something to blame. And that something fastens on Morgan. He vows to "run from the wild woods where wandered Morgan le Fay, seeking him with enchantments and spells" (136), but his newly awakened instincts overcome the control which has held them in check, as he forgets Marlingate in his adulterous love affair with Morgan.

And the love affair liberates his repressions. He feels a reality he has never known. The vague feeling of "a reach beyond, which had always qualified his relations with the town had now departed. . . . surprisingly he stood closer than ever to Marlingate" (130). He is in a lover's (and a fool's) paradise. But while it lasts, his nature blossoms: he opens his heart and his house; the people of the town marvel at his new geniality. He has the best of both of his worlds. "The Mayor of Marlingate had his secret place in the woods, where he could dance and tumble on the brown leaves without shame, and forget without loss or guilt the red town behind the tamarisks" (141).

Even the woods threaten him no longer, for he is one with nature, one with eternity. "He no longer had that feeling of hostility towards the woods, for in them, as it were, the scrolls and deeds of his lover were deposited. . . . He liked to think of those two great freedoms outside his town, sighing and straining to each other across it, linking themselves with winds that

fluttered and sped, ignoring the blot of crimson dust between"
(144-45). Marlingate, town of the tamarisks, the epitome of his
dream, has become for him a "blot of crimson dust."

Monypenny's blending of the opposing forces of his nature into
an ecstatic harmony does not eradicate, however, his innate
snobbishness. He knows that he loves Morgan not only because
she enchants him, but because she has the gentility he cherishes,
gentility she has cultivated to win his love.

The flowering of his nature in love leads Monypenny to
develop a conscience. Before, his concern centered on conventions, what people would think of him. Now, paradoxically,
through sinning against Becket by loving Becket's wife,
Monypenny realizes that Becket is a human being, not the
instrument he has used to his own ends. He sees Becket linked to
him in a common humanity. "Was it true that we were all linked
up by our mutual wrongs, our common struggles, our
forgivenesses? . . . . a world wider than Marlingate seemed to
open, a grey world in a half light, where men sinned sadly and
unwillingly against each other and as sadly and willingly forgave,
where black and white and light and darkness were all smudged
together in one grey blur of tears, tears of sorrow, tears of
pardon" (158).

Through releasing the humanizing power of his natural
emotions and passions, Monypenny has learned wisdom. He has
matured to the point of seeing himself as a human being, not as a
king. His newfound conscience tells him that he is behaving in a
way that makes him hurt people, Becket first of all (although
Becket does not realize that his wife is unfaithful to him); then
Fanny Vidler, whom Monypenny is courting and using as a shield
for his actions; then Fanny's uncle, Vidler, who trusts him as
being a person of honor.

The town's need precipitates a decision. He needs money from
Becket for a venture which is connected with the success of
Marlingate, but he knows that to ask Becket for it will be to act in
such a way that it would be "an outrage to all decent feeling"
(159). For a year he has been enjoying both Morgan and
Marlingate, but the situation can no longer be tolerated. His
awakened consciousness will not allow it. He must make a choice.
To run off with Morgan, as she wishes, would result in a scandal
which would lose him Marlingate. To give up Morgan would

mean giving up part of himself. "Which of these two dear things could he forsake? — the town which was his own creation or the woman whose new creation he was. He had made Marlingate a town and Morgan had made him a man" (172).

Yet he recognizes that both Marlingate and Morgan are part of himself. He knows that the town is "built of the stuff of his dreams, of his own substance, of his own soul." When he realizes that he must renounce it "in its perfections," he feels his "love for it returning as a sickness of which he must die" (177). And he chooses the town, for "the spell of its illusions had proved stronger than the spell of her flesh and blood" (189). Trapped in the dream, he forgoes reality for illusion.

Morgan cannot sustain life without Monypenny, for she has made herself over for him. She has "renounced her own nature, but he had not given her his, so she was indeed for his sake without a soul, a weak, helpless, drifting thing, foam upon the water" (192). For the first time she sees Monypenny's love for his town as real, understanding that it is part of him as her love for him is part of her. Because she feels that she has not only lost Monypenny but herself as well, she throws herself over the cliff, convinced that although he "had found his youth and his manhood in her . . . her love had become a snare to him, and in a little while it would become a sorrow" (196).

Although Monypenny feels a curious relief at hearing the news of Morgan's death, feeling "the lifting of a yoke and the removal of a snare" (204), the feeling is short-lived, for he soon realizes that he "had built Marlingate for Morgan — before he had ever seen her he had built it for her — she was that Dream Beyond, after which he had always striven, and at last had held, and now had slain" (220). He knows that he has killed the best part of himself, the part represented by Morgan and her love. The Dionysian revel is over, and there are just the bitter dregs of remorse and sorrow, and the piper to pay. Morgan was his destiny. In accepting her and the passion she represented, he could have had Marlingate, but "when he renounced Morgan, he lost Marlingate too. . . . she had taken his town with her into the shadows. Marlingate was dead" (221).

Tragedy has opened his eyes. He learns, too late, that the denial of his nature, the refusal to face the reality of his being, has brought him pain and suffering. But it has not brought him the wisdom he needs. He is no Oedipus, accepting punishment in the knowledge that he has gained a greater wisdom. Instead, the struggle for power over himself and others now springs forth renewed, and he must smash that which he once created out of his own substance. In destroying Marlingate, he will destroy himself. He rationalizes, in his frustration and anger, blaming Morgan for the destruction he will wreak on Marlingate. "He had built his town for her, and then had offered her up as a sacrifice to it. Nothing less than its ruin could avenge her, nor her monument be less than the defiled stones on which he, poor betrayed priest of the Golden Bough, had offered her to an illusion" (267).

The creativity of destruction takes the place of the creativity of construction. Systematically, he destroys the town, cleverly suggesting plans through which it will deteriorate into a seedy resort. And as the years pass, Monypenny learns nothing further. With the death of Morgan, he loses his chance at full maturity as a human being. His failure as a husband to Fanny Vidler, his failure as a father to Ted, his failure to those town councilmen who believe in him and back him with their money—all these serve the destruction of the town, the only thing that will satisfy him.

Yet, Monypenny feels himself a success. He feels the surge of power within himself, although he blinds himself to its source:

Any man with wealth and energy and enterprise could boom a decent village into a fashionable resort, but one had to be more than wealthy and enterprising to work the charm backwards. One had to be damn clever. . . . It had been a long and terrible job, and in the process of it he had lost all that he had still left to lose—his wife, his son, his fortune, his health. . . . he had won his victory; for he had vindicated his manhood in the face of the grinding forces of earth and had shown himself able to destroy the work of his own hands when that work had become vile. (331)

He feels that "by vengeance he had purged his soul of its error" (351). As he had lived an illusion through his dream for Marlingate (his soul's error), he has now destroyed that illusion through the destruction of Marlingate.

His "vengeance" avenges itself on him, as he dies of the wound from the stone thrown at him by one of the rowdy mob. In a final irony, words spoken at the unveiling of his statue sum up, literally, his life: "Marlingate is the monument of this great and noble man, it is his life's work, and the work for which he gave his life" (380). The turnabout of everything for which Monypenny fought and dreamed results in a life work ending in vengeance, the selling out of his ideals as well as the selling out of those who supported him in these ideals. And the final words of the novel sum up the basic theme. "Only the great statue of Monypenny stood blocked against the sunset, staring with blind eyes out to sea" (386).

The statue is larger than life, as Monypenny hoped to be—in fact, had thought himself to be. Its blind eyes symbolize Monypenny's blindness to everyone and everything except himself. His egocentricity, his failure to realize both his responsibility toward, and his community with, his fellow human beings, brings him to the end of his life as he had lived his life—blind. He had a chance at maturity when his conscience first began to prod him, when he felt the liberating power of his love for Morgan. But he lost this chance when he failed to overcome his need for conventional respectability and municipal honors.

The novel works on many levels A review in the *Times Literary Supplement* states that *Tamarisk Town* is the story "of a man who in youth sacrifices the spiritual side of his life to the material."[12] Yet the obvious level of material versus spiritual values appears only sporadically. Monypenny is a divided soul, seeking wholeness, forced toward wholeness, but prevented from achieving it by his blind self-interest. Wishing to stem the tide of time and eternity, he stands as Everyman, helpless against powers arraigned against him. These powers are symbolized by the woods and the sea. As he attempts to overcome these powers, he finds himself first caught up in them and then a willing ally of them.

His surge upward to the power he craves fails to satisfy his basic longing. He learns too late that love could have been his answer. The forces arrayed against him are formidable, for they are eternal, while he is mortal. Failing to embrace the one activity which could have saved him—loving Morgan and surrendering himself to her in communion with her and, therefore, community with others—there remains nothing left for him but to destroy. And the destruction of Marlingate is his own destruction.

Sheila Kaye-Smith neither condemns nor applauds Monypenny's actions. She presents him as an introspective egocentric, rationalizing away responsibility for his actions. The creative force which could have been released through his love for Morgan is cut off by his desire for power. Yet in creating Marlingate as a place of beauty, he had created himself. But this was not enough, just as the aesthetic impulse is only the beginning.[13] He stepped into the ethical stage when he began to consider his actions in relation to their effect on others. But he never reached the moral level. And his ethics are not strong enough to withstand the knowledge of the evil he has done. He slides backward into his need for power, his need to prove himself to himself, in the same way that Reuben Backfield has to prove himself to himself. For Backfield, the proof is sufficient. For Monypenny it is not, undoubtedly because Monypenny reaches an ethical level of action, while Backfield does not.

Both *Tamarisk Town* and *Sussex Gorse* depend greatly on physical areas for atmosphere and conflict. Boarzell Moor and Tamarisk Town are treated as entities which have human characteristics. As such, they must be tamed, civilized, brought into productive use. And those who do the taming create themselves along with their creations. Backfield is satisfied with what he has made and with himself; Monypenny is dissatisfied both with his creation and with himself.

Both novels tell about the thought processes of the protagonists rather than presenting action. This slows the novels down and tends to make them repetitive. But on the deepest level, both novels speak not only to the destructive use of power, but also to the human condition which dares more than it can hope to obtain, and in the daring loses that which makes it human—the recognition of itself as a loving creature.

CHAPTER 3

Struggling Women

MANY critics point out that Sheila Kaye-Smith writes like a man. One states that, although he wonders whether or not it is a compliment, he "should not be surprised if a reader of, say 'Starbrace' or 'Sussex Gorse' were to think that Sheila Kaye-Smith is the pen name of a man."[1] Another writes that she is "masculine in her outlook."[2] It is also said that one won't enjoy her if one "doesn't like women writers who talk like men."[3] Cornelius Weygandt points out that the "man-like attitude of Sheila Kaye-Smith has led certain critics to wonder whether the author of the books so signed was not a man writing under a woman's name."[4] This criticism, and it is only a sampling of much on the same subject, stems from a time at which a clear dichotomy existed between men and women novelists. The critics apparently assumed that they were paying Miss Kaye-Smith a compliment, although one of them has the grace to wonder about this.

It must be remembered that "for most of man's history it had been believed that the capacity for learning and mental creativity was unique to men. . . . so far as was understood, the head was the organ men had for mental creation, whereas the womb was the organ women had for physical creation. It was a matter of either/or."[5] For the Victorians, and the tradition lingered into the first half of the twentieth century, if indeed it still does not linger,[6] the categories that Victorian periodical reviewing were based on were that "women writers were acknowledged to possess sentiment, refinement, tact, observation, domestic expertise, high moral tone, and knowledge of female character; and thought to lack originality, intellectual training, abstract intelligence, humor, self-control, and knowledge of male character. Male writers had most of the desirable qualities: power, breadth, distinctness, clarity, learning, abstract intelligence, shrewdness, experience, humor, knowledge of everyone's character, and open-mindedness."[7]

The critics who point out that Sheila Kaye-Smith "writes like a man," appear to be saying that she shows the qualities inherent in good writing (qualities almost exclusively attributed to men at that time). It is sufficient to point out here that she does indeed exhibit these qualities. It must at the same time be forcibly stated that the criticism is sexist in nature and that women novelists have suffered enormously from it and are still suffering from it.[8]

As the classification of writers into "men" and "women" novelists is disappearing, the question of whether Sheila Kaye-Smith writes like a man or like a women is not pertinent. This study points out her strengths and her weaknesses, none of which belong exclusively to one sex or the other. It must be noted, however, that in her society, and therefore in the society she presents in her novels, certain human characteristics were labeled "feminine" or "masculine," depending on the expectations of the society.[9]

Two characters in novels which bear their names, Joanna Godden and Susan Spray, both accede to, and rebel against, these manmade expectations of their society. In these novels, Miss Kaye-Smith creates strong, rebellious women, but the women exhibit differing personalities and are informed by different visions of existence. Both triumph over their condition; both refuse to accept their limitations as "feminine;" but Joanna Godden becomes a woman of courage and of maturity, while Susan Spray remains a woman of superstition and of hypocrisy. But both struggle desperately. In considering the struggle and the motivation for it in each novel, the reader gains insight not only into the mind of Sheila Kaye-Smith, but also into universal characteristics of human beings.

One of the most memorable, and one of the most popular, of Miss Kaye-Smith's characters is Joanna Godden. None of her women characters have received so much critical acclaim.[10] Robert Thurston Hopkins calls *Joanna Godden* her "best novel."[11] Elizabeth Drew feels that Joanna Godden shares with Rueben Backfield the honor of being her "greatest artistic achievement," because in these two characters, she created the "spirit of the land."[12] She calls *Joanna Godden* "the epic of a woman's strength, of the stability and steadfastness of character which incarnates the vitality and simpleness of the land itself."[13]

In addition, J. R. N. Maxwell writes that "no character she has drawn has ever equalled this creation. Strength and weakness, unselfish love and generous self-sacrifice all clamor for predominance in Joanna."[14]

Continuing the acclaim, Mother M. Agatha finds *Joanna Godden* a novel in which one finds Sheila Kaye-Smith's "magnificent intuitive power."[15] And Margaret Mackenzie chooses *Joanna Godden* as a close second to *Green Apple Harvest* as her favorite of Sheila Kaye-Smith's novels.[16] The foregoing represents only a sampling of the accolades heaped on *Joanna Godden*.

Sheila Kaye-Smith has made Joanna Godden "a woman very much after her own heart" according to Fletcher Allen.[17] For this reason, a study of *Joanna Godden* reveals Miss Kaye-Smith's ideas of, and ideals for, women. In most of her other novels, women characters take the usual-in-fiction position of acting as foils to men, serving them and helping (or hindering) them to achieve their desire. The women in *Sussex Gorse* pale beside Reuben Backfield. He uses them to further his ambition, and they, for the most part, accept his commands, as does Naomi, or escape his jurisdiction, as does Rose. Alice Jury appears as a complete woman, but her relationship with Backfield forms only a minute part of the novel.

Morgan Wells of *Tamarisk Town,* although called her "favorite" by G. B. Stern[18] resembles more the fantasy woman of English and American literature than a flesh and blood heroine. Pictured as an "enchantress," willing to give up home, husband, and children for her lover, making herself into what her lover wants, and eventually killing herself for his sake, Morgan Wells stands not only for the Dionysian side of Monypenny but also for the masculine ideal of what a woman should be.

Joanna Godden remains, then, not only a rarity in fiction, but a rarity in life, at least in life as it was when the novel first appeared. Patrick Braybrooke, in a book written in 1931, calls Joanna Godden an "intensely modern woman in an era when such creatures were but rare."[19] He finds her "rather like Reuben [Backfield]. She will rule with a rod of iron, but a woman's ruling is more likely to be bent."[20] There is none of Braybrooke's chauvinism present in Sheila Kaye-Smith. Her characters appear as people who happen to be of one sex or the other. This is not to imply that they (and she) are not affected by the mores of their society, the conventions which help or inhibit their desires and give them the motivations for action. But the characteristics of her protagonists are rooted in human beings of both sexes. This gives her art the universality which brings it into the realm of literature.

I Joanna Godden

Like Reuben Backfield and Edward Monypenny, Joanna Godden struggles to form herself into a mature human being, but unlike them, she is not hampered by the deep insecurity which makes their struggle destructive. She begins, and she ends, as a warm, caring, courageous human being who happens to be a woman. And she ends, through her struggles, as a freer being. The fact that she is a woman limits her actions, but it frees her emotions. Of the three, she becomes not only the happiest, but the most fulfilled.

Joanna's story begins toward the middle of October 1897, with the funeral of her father. Joanna, twenty-three years old, is left with Ansdore, her father's fairly prosperous farm, and her ten year old sister, Ellen. Because she has always helped her father farm, the running of the farm presents no problems to her; in fact, it gives her the opportunity to try new ideas. After some setbacks, she makes the farm, and herself, extremely prosperous. She sends Ellen to a good school to become what she calls "a lady." Joanna, although uneducated, attracts, through her persistence, the attention of the squire's son, Martin. Martin, well-educated, genteel, and "a gentleman" falls in love with Joanna, and she with him. Martin exhibits many of the "feminine" traits of the time, such as gentleness, while Joanna exhibits many of the "masculine" ones, such as aggressiveness. Together they make up an androgynous ideal. But Martin, never physically strong, dies just before their planned marriage, leaving a void in Joanna's life.

After Ellen completes her education, Joanna persuades Arthur Alce, her own loyal beau, to marry Ellen. Ellen marries Arthur to escape Joanna's domination, and Arthur marries Ellen because he cannot refuse Joanna anything. They live a fairly happy life for a while. Then Ellen becomes restless, bored with country life, and runs off with the squire, a man old enough to be her father. After a time, Ellen realizes that Arthur will not divorce her,

and she comes home to Joanna who, meanwhile, has built up her
holdings, acquired new land, including the squire's, and become
the "squire." Ellen eventually meets a gentleman, Tip Ernley,
and plans to marry him. Joanna is pleased that Ellen will finally
become the "lady" she has so long wanted her to be.

Joanna, overworked and restless, goes to Marlingate[21] for a
rest. She picks up a rather unscrupulous young man, Albert Hill, a
man thirteen years her junior. The unsatisfied longings of many
years compel her to enter into an intimate love affair with Bertie
(Albert Hill). Her strict conscience, however, prods her into
insisting that they sanctify their affair through marriage. Bertie
consents, realizing that Joanna is both rich and attractive. While
visiting his home to meet his mother and sister, Joanna sees
Bertie for what he is, a selfish, uncaring person. She realizes that
she could not bear to live with him, and she breaks off the
engagement.

On the train on her way home, Joanna feels life stirring within
her, and she realizes that she is carrying Bertie's child. Elated
and distressed at the same time, she tells a horrified Ellen the
situation. To spare Ellen embarrassment, and to protect her
child's life from mean gossips, Joanna decides to leave her
beloved farm. Her story ends as she goes forth to face the future
with her customary courage.[22]

II   *Emergence of Self*

Unlike Reuben Backfield *(Sussex Gorse)* and Edward
Monypenny *(Tamarisk Town)*, Joanna Godden has no "goal," no
"dream," no impetus to action through which she must transcend
selfhood. She loves the farm that she has been brought up on,
and she enjoys taking care of it, making a living from it for herself
and Ellen. To do this, she must assume some of the prerogatives
of men, and she does so willingly, not because she wants to be a
man, but because she wants the privileges men enjoy. She has, at
the very beginning of her story, a "vague sorrow"[23] which she
attributes to her father's death. This "vague sorrow" comes upon
her at various stages of her life, however, so that her life does not
provide her with complete fulfillment as she does what she feels
she should. Rather, she searches for she knows not what. This
"vague sorrow" leaves her only when she knows that she carries
a child.

Despite Sheila Kaye-Smith's stressing of the conventional fulfillment of a woman through love, marriage, and child-bearing in *Joanna Godden,* Joanna stands outside the idea of a conventional heroine. Like Becky Sharpe in *Vanity Fair* and Elizabeth Bennet in *Pride and Prejudice* she is a protagonist, a "hero," a person who causes actions and who responds with daring to those actions. When faced with the task of running the farm, she takes over the task of hiring, firing, and supervising the men. She knows that she is quite equal to the task. She does not shirk going to market, nor does she shirk working alongside her hired hands to make sure that they give a full day's work. Yet taking over a man's job does not lessen her conviction that social attitudes must be maintained. Unconventional though her ideas may be, both in her dress and in her running of the farm, "she would as soon have thought of jumping out of the window as of discarding her mourning a day before the traditions of the Marsh decreed" (22). Even though "her values demanded that she should be slightly more splendid in church than at market . . . she knew that folks would stare, so she might as well give them something to stare at" (22). This defiance in the midst of conventional behavior makes Joanna a very human woman. She struggles to remove herself from the straight-laced ideas of the farming community, but she refuses, at the same time, to remove herself from her straight-laced stays.

When loyal, dutiful Alfred Alcye gently remonstrates with her that she does things out of place in a woman (changing the accepted methods of farming, painting her house and her carriage other colors than those usual, scolding her looker (herdsman) in the middle of Lydd Market), Joanna treats his objections with "good-humored, almost tender, indifference" (25). When Alfred further remonstrates that she ought to spend her time with women talk, "puddings and stuffing mattresses and such-like women's subjects," she tells him, "I talk about them too and I can't see as I'd be any better for talking of nothing else" (25).

Joanna struggles, not to be a man, but to be a woman with a man's prerogative to act beyond the domestic sphere. She needs to assert herself, needs to feel that her knowledge extends to those concerns which, in her community, belong strictly to men. Not only does she wish to know, but she wishes to display her knowledge, even though the men of the town resent her aggressive behavior and criticize her hiring of Socknersh as looker, grumbling that "maybe she'd sooner have a looker as knew nothing, and then she could teach him" (29). But Joanna's choice of the slow-witted Socknersh is not based solely on her ability to dominate him, although that is a serious consideration, but rather, his slow-witted nature "stirred something with her that was almost tender" (30). Like the traditional women in literature, Joanna Godden looks for someone to love, someone on whom to spend her service and her compassion. She hires Socknersh, then, because she likes him best and because he "would mind her properly and take to her ways" (31).

Her struggle to gain an outlet for her creativity centers on those things available to a woman: her wagons, which become "like mad galleys of a bye-gone age"; her clothes, which become flamboyant in style and color; and the decoration of Ellen's room, an outlandish riot of color. She needs to assert her personality, to show that she counts for something. Her improvements give her a "sense of adventurous satisfaction." The yellow doors and windows on her house, her boldly designed window curtains, her "high pooped waggons," the brass-buttoned uniform that her coachman wears—"all appealed to something fundamental in her which was big and boastful" (35). She even enjoys being the center of all eyes as she drives into town, and she relishes the gossip that she causes.

Socknersh, good-looking although slow-witted, becomes the object of Joanna's sexual desire, even though she insists that she keeps him on because he obeys her loyally. She is torn between her natural desire for love and for sexual fulfillment on one hand and her desire that these must be sought with someone she can admire, respect, and feel equal to on the other. When she is overjoyed to find that it is not Socknersh who made pregnant her chicken girl, her good sense makes her look at the actions precipitated by her need for affection. Although she assures herself that it doesn't matter what people think of her, she knows that their opinion mirrors her own. She forces herself to honesty as she fires the bewildered Socknersh. She cries because "she was humbled in her own eyes." She had kept Socknersh on for two years, knowing his ignorance and his inefficiency, "simply because his strength and good looks had enslaved her susceptible womanhood" (63-64).

She is horrified that "mere youth and comeliness and virility should blind her judgment and strip her of common sense. Yet this was obviously the lesson she must learn." And learning the lesson, she cries, "Oh God! . . . why didn't you make me a man?" (65). But Joanna wants the freedom of b⸍ ᵓg a man, tʰ freedom to find her satisfactions as men do. H ⸴ v ᵓmanhoᶜ restricts her to actions that she accepts because ᶜf society ⸴ mores, even though they limit her freedom. Caught between her natural instinct for freedom and her conviction that conventional behavior is right behavior, Joanna struggles for a compromise.

Joanna's freedom is limited by the idea that being married is the only important fact in a woman's life. She "despised" ladies with letters after their names, because she felt sure that "they had never had a chance of getting married" (70). But beneath all her plans that Ellen must go to school to become a "lady," there is no hint that she, herself, feels inferior to her sister. Quite the contrary. Ellen does not care for Ansdore. She shall not grow up like her sister "in capable commonness." So "half-unconsciously," she plans that Ellen shall wear rich clothes and idle her time away while she herself "ventured and toiled." Ellen's lot is to be the "happiest lot she could picture for anyone, though she would have loathed it herself" (70).

The attitude reminds one of the doers of the world who enjoy planning a life of nondoing for others, knowing full well that the nondoers will have a lesser life. Joanna plans, for others as well as for herself. And she convinces herself that she is doing her best for Ellen. Even though the two sisters are opposite in needs and motivations, they love each other.

Joanna, although strong, sturdy, big, colorful, and courageous, still needs the respect of others, for it is through their respect that she can respect herself. She does not rebel against the opinion of her neighbors; rather, she rebels against the restrictions of her sex. In overcoming these restrictions, she still requires the approval of others. "She was proud of what she had done for her little sister, and she was proud, too, of having restored Ansdore to prosperity. . . . She knew that the neighbors were impressed by Ansdore's thriving when they had foretold its downfall under her sway. . . . She had vindicated her place in her father's shoes . . . she had expiated her folly in the matter of Socknersh, and restored her credit not only in the bar of the Woolpack, but in her own eyes" (72-72).

Joanna's compassionate nature reveals itself in her ability to

put herself in the other person's place. Realizing how embarrass-
ing it must be for Mr. Pratt, the timid parson, to beg money for a
new organ from his parishioners, she writes a check for the full
amount needed; firing Socknersh to ease her conscience, she
pays him until he has another position; dismissing her hired girl
who is pregnant out of wedlock, she pays for the wedding and
her lying in month afterward. But Joanna does not make much of
these charitable acts. Actually, they seem to embarrass her.
When she writes the check for Mr. Pratt, her cheeks burn "with
a queer kind of shame" (75).

But she feels no shame in taking over the position of a man in
farming Ansdore. And she must battle the prejudice of her fellow
farmers, who never let her forget that she is a woman and not
one of them. They allow her, grudgingly, to attend the Farmers'
Club dinner, where she is the only woman present, but they do
not invite her to join the club itself. She "swings" through the
dinner, an occasion into which "most women would have crept"
(78). She is even proud to be there, as she pictures the farmers'
wives questioning their husbands about her afterwards. Vennal,
one of the members, sums up the men's attitude as he proclaims,
"I don't hold for a woman to have pluck. . . . Pluck makes a
woman think she can do without a man." And no matter how she
might impress the members with her daring and her knowledge
of farming, she is only a guest, and the men would "far rather
open those doors ceremonially now and then than allow her to go
freely in and out" (83-84).[24]

Thus Joanna is effectively locked out of the world in which she
has, by dint of hard work and courage, earned a share, for the
inhabitants of this world force her to keep to the place which
they feel is proper for a woman. Yet so strong has been her
conditioning, and so strong are her needs for love and
companionship, that she believes that her dissatisfaction occurs
only because she does not have a home with a husband and
children. These are the highest priorities of her vision. She
believes that women are very different from men, "even if they
did the same things." Women's sphere to her means a husband
and children. And if you had a husband and children, "you didn't
go knocking at the men's doors, but shut yourself snugly inside
your own. . . . But if you were alone inside your room . . . then
it was terrible, worse than being outside . . . and no wonder you
went around to the men's doors . . . and begged them to give

you a little company, or something to do to help you forget your empty room" (84).

Joanna Godden, product of a manmade society which locks out women, conditioned to accept the romantic notions of marriage, realizes that marriage alone will not solve her loneliness. She must have a perfect mate so that her marriage will be a "big, romantic adventure — she wanted either to marry someone above herself in birth and station, or else very much below" (85). Thus, Joanna must either serve in slavish devotion to someone she looks up to or serve in slavish devotion to a child or a childlike person, a person like Socknersh. But her devotion to Socknersh has proved stultifying. Caught in the trap of love and service, she can only try what she has not yet experienced, love with a person of higher station than she.

Luckily for her, the notice of Martin Trevor, son of the squire, a man "dark, tall, well-born, comely and strong of frame, and yet with that hidden delicacy, that weakness which Joanna must have in a man if she was to love him" (85), supplies her need. The hidden delicacy and weakness are qualities ordinarily described by her society as "feminine." Joanna, then, must have a man who is androgynous, one who embodies the best qualities of those ordinarily assigned to each sex. Martin Trevor has another "feminine" quality which Joanna prizes — inexperience. As she struggles to help herself emerge as the forceful, dynamic being she knows she can become, she cannot tolerate a man who lords it over her. Her constant assertion of her own superiority, particularly in matters of sheep-raising, attests to her need for self-definition.

Although Joanna thinks of taking a husband in the terms of hiring a farmhand, giving service for benefits received, her love for Martin and his for her are sincere and deep. Martin is astute enough to see her "bustle and self-confidence" as something "rather pathetic, a mere trapping of feminine weakness. . . . Under her loud voice, her almost barbaric appearance, her queerly truculent manner, was a naive mixture of child and woman — soft, simple, eager to please" (90). And because he finds in her an "unsuspected streak of goodness, a sound, sweet core which he had not looked for under his paradox of softness and brutality. . . ," he concludes that it would be "worth while committing himself with Joanna Godden" (99).

Through her love for Martin, Joanna experiences the paradox

of love. One part of her recognizes that his love will satisfy her craving; the other part of her knows that in marrying him, she will be giving up part of herself, enslaving herself. At the time she was enamoured with Socknersh, she had looked into Socknersh's eyes and seen a tiny image of herself. At the height of her happiness with Martin, it is this image which comes back to haunt her. "A memory smote her—of herself standing before another man who blocked the sky, and in whose eyes sat the small, enslaved image of herself. . . . Ought she to draw back while she had still the power, before she became his slave, his little thing, and all her bigness was drowned in his eyes. She knew that whatever she gave him now could never be taken back. Here stood the master of the mistress of Ansdore" (105-106). Although the warning strikes her, warns her that in marrying Martin she will lose irrevocably something of her potentiality, she falls into the trap of love and stills the warning. And she changes, for "something in her was broken, melted, changed out of all recognition—she was softer, weaker, more excited, more tender. She had lost some of her old cocksureness, for Martin had utterly surprised and tamed her" (112).

The warning that Martin receives as he shrinks from becoming "Mr. Joanna Godden" (115) resides more in what the townspeople will think of him than in any threat to his own individuality. Unlike Joanna's certainty that in marrying him "all her bigness" would be gone, he feels that their differences are gifts for them to give each other: "he brought her gifts of knowledge and imagination and emotion, and she brought him gifts of stability and simplicity and a certain saving commonness" (119).

Joanna fully accepts her subservience to Martin's desires and needs, as she sees that "even right could surrender. . . . her plans, her ambitions, her life, herself, had their worth only in the knowledge that they belonged to him" (130). But due to Martin's death, her subservience is short-lived, although the road to a reidentification of herself with her activities does not come easily. Even though Ansdore calls to her to "come back. . . . I'm all you've got now" (144), she is "just flying and rattling about like a broken thing" (148). For Martin had shown her "a vision of herself as complete woman, mother and wife, of a Joanna Godden bigger than Ansdore" (149). Thus Joanna still lives in romantic illusion, forgetting the warning, forgetting the "slave" nature of the hoped for relationship.

Even though part of Joanna sees life through the illusion of romance, part of her meets life with practical common sense. This common sense stands her in good stead when her romantic dreams die with Martin. Through her work at Ansdore, she slowly begins to value her single state, which begins to have "a certain worth in itself, a respectable rigour like a pair of stays" (163). The value she puts on her single self prevents her from marrying Arthur Alce, but she has not yet conquered fully her idea that destiny for a woman is marriage. Although she finds satisfaction in arranging Ellen's marriage to Arthur, she still feels a vague longing, a sense that life passes her by. "Sometimes she would be overwhelmed, in the midst of all her triumphant business, with a sense of personal failure. She had succeeded where most women are hopeless failures, but where so many women are successful and satisfied, she had failed and gone empty" (219).

Even when Ellen disgraces her by running off with Squire Trevor, Joanna sometimes feels, not a sense of judgment toward Ellen, but envy. She feels, sometimes, that "she would like to see all the fullness of her life at Ansdore, all her honour on the three marshes, blown to the winds if only in their stead she could have just ordinary human love, with or without the law" (220). This is a large turnabout for the Joanna who values respectability above all. Ambivalent now towards those things which had always been her props—Ansdore, and the respect of her neighbors—she finds her old fighting spirit failing. She is ripe for her love affair with Bertie Hill, for to her he represents the lost romance of her dead lover, Martin, and a second chance at her dream. It is "his youth she wanted most partly because it called to something in her . . . which had never yet been satisfied" (280). He is, to her, "all things—fulfillment, lover and child, and also a Sign and a Second Coming" (289). Ansdore is not enough for her to devote her life to. It was failing her "as it always failed her in any crisis of emotion—Ansdore could never be big enough to fill her heart" (288).

She feels herself a queen inviting Bertie, as consort, to share her throne. Yet she knows that "in outward circumstances she was his queen, but in her heart she was his slave" (288). And as his slave, she accedes to his demands for intimacy. He is her little boy, and she is gratifying his desires and at the same time her own. A complete joy in her sexual surrender fails to materialize, as it carries with it the guilt of trodden on commandments. She realizes that she is a sinner, like Ellen and those others whose actions she formerly condemned.

Marriage "alone could hallow and remake Joanna Godden." At times, away from the power of physical love, "her thoughts awoke, and she would be overwhelmed by an almost incredulous horror at herself" (307). She knows now that no actions of others will ever shock her, for she sees herself as worse than anyone she knows.

Like Reuben Backfield and Edward Monypenny, Joanna Godden places the responsibility for her actions outside her own emotion and will. As Backfield blamed Boarzell and Monypenny blamed Marlingate, she blames "life," which is "queer," taking a person "by surprise in a way you'd never think—it made you do things so different from your proper notions that afterwards you could hardly believe it was you that had done them—it gave you joy that should ought to have been sorrow. . . and pain as you'd never think" (307).

But the joy and the pain make Joanna into both a perceptive and an honest person. She has the strength and courage to give up Bertie when she sees his small-mindedness and his selfishness. Also, her heightened awareness makes her realize that their marriage would put him in prison as well as put her there. She pities him, for he is "no strong man, no lover and husband—just a little clerk she was going to shut up in prison. . . . She felt a brute" (323).

Despite the fact that only marriage with Bertie will cleanse her and give her back her self-respect, she knows she can never marry him. She must "just do without respecting herself. . . . Anything would be better than shutting up herself and Albert together in prison, till they hated each other. . . . Well, she'd do her best, and perhaps God would forgive her" (334–35).

Even when she discovers she is carrying Bertie's child, her resolution does not falter. It becomes stronger, and convinced of the rightness of her decision, she experiences joy. Fearful and joyful at the same time, her courage reaches its greatest height, for "as the joy grew and rose above the fear, she knew that she could never let fear drive her into bondage" (338). She stands, then a courageous woman, overcoming her fear of society's censure with the knowledge that she will finally have what she has always wanted—a child.

Although it will be "the worst, most shattering thing she had ever yet endured," she will endure it for the sake of her love for the child she carries. She sees now that although she had tried to fill her life with work, her sister, men, "what she had always wanted had been a child" (338).

The emotional release caused by her vow to give herself in love to her unborn child convinces her that Ansdore has been only a substitute for what she really wanted. It is all past now, "all her ambition, all her success, all the greatness of Joanna Godden. She had made Ansdore great and prosperous though she was a woman, and then she had lost it, because she was a woman," but she finds the thought of Ansdore fading in her mind "as it had always faded in the presence of any vital instinct, whether of love or death." And "none of her men, except perhaps Martin could have been to her what her child would be" (344).

Joanna Godden here reveals herself as still the romantic, still the starry-eyed server of a loved one. But she gains more than a feeling of joy. She gains a release for her repression of the idea of Martin's death, for "now strange barriers of thought had broken down, and she seemed to go to and fro quite easily into the past. . . . She was free to remember all their going out and coming in together. . . . Throughout her being there was a strange sense of release—broken, utterly done and finished as she was from the wordly point of view, there was in her heart a springing hope, a sweet softness—she could indeed go softly at last" (345).

Throwing all into the hopper of her love for her unborn child, Joanna can now face both the past and the future. She can gain comfort by thinking of Martin. She stands, nearly forty, facing a new life. She has lost all that she formerly valued: "her lover, her sister, her farm, her home, her good name." But "the past and the future still were hers" (353).

Joanna Godden stands a strong, courageous woman, winning her struggle to overcome the demands of a society which fails to support her need for individuality. Defiant, refusing to accept the place which society allocates to a woman, she fights, through sheer energy and determination, to win respect of the men she respects. Although accepted in her independence and in her ability by these men, she is betrayed, according to Sheila Kaye-Smith, by her womanhood. As presented, Joanna Godden remains a contradiction. Exhibiting the feminine qualities of a Victorian heroine—service in love, subordination to men, and acceptance of conventional mores—she also exhibits an impatience with these qualities and struggles beyond them. Yet her emotions force her into the feminine mold, and she joyfully accepts the diminishing of herself, not for love of a husband, but for love of a child. One can only pity the child who must bear such a burden of love.

Yet, paradoxically, through her struggles, she emerges as a complete human being, willing to forgo what had heretofore meant the most to her—Ansdore, her sister, a respectable married life—because she knows that forcing herself into the conventional mold will ruin the chances for her child. Life, for Joanna Godden, is loving and serving. Unlike Reuben Backfield and Edward Monypenny, Joanna does not seek to go beyond her humanity. She seeks to fulfill it. As she vows to go on living to the fullest through the serving of the child she carries, she has stripped herself of the pettiness of pride and envy which heretofore clouded her vision. She stands secure in the knowledge of who she is and what she stands for. She is a mature woman, and she stands for courage and hope.

III   Susan Spray

Another of Sheila Kaye-Smith's strong women, Susan Spray, also finds herself victim of a man's world. Susan Spray, prophet-teacher, whose story is told in the novel which bears her name, attempts, like Reuben Backfield and Edward Monypenny, to overcome her humanity. But in addition, like Joanna Godden, she also struggles to step out of the place in society which men have made for women. Her colossal ego aligns itself with Deity itself, as her struggle, like Joanna Godden's, leads to strength on the one hand, but like Reuben Backfield's, leads to the weakness of self-deception on the other. Unlike Joanna Godden, Susan Spray rejects the idea that she must find her place in society. While Joanna accepts with reluctance her conventional role, Susan refuses to compromise. Her story ends, as it begins, with her rebellion.

At the beginning of the novel, the reader learns that Susan Spray was born in 1834 to a very poor family of farm laborers, at Copthorne, which is a town on the Surrey and Sussex borders. The family is so poor that the children, of whom Susan is the eldest, are sent out to work in the fields. Children of three years of age and upward are sent out to earn a few pennies by picking stones from the field or scaring away birds. Into this poverty-stricken family are born seven more children until, worn out with child bearing and with hunger, Mrs. Spray dies.

The family belongs to the Colgate Brotherhood, a sect founded by Hur Colgate some years before. The tenets of this religion resemble High Calvinism, the religion their founder had left in order to found the Colgate Brotherhood. Susan's entire education consists of learning to read the Bible which, as an imaginative child, she takes literally. To pass the time she must spend in the hated fields, she tells herself stories, all based on biblical events.

One day, frightened home by a severe thunderstorm, she relates that she has seen God. She tells of her vision both because she half believes it and also because she hopes that by telling her parents that God ordered her home, she will escape a beating for leaving her job. The repetition of her "vision" before the brotherhood gives her a prominence which eventually starts her on her road to preaching and prophesy. On the death of both parents, she spends some time in a workhouse, after being taken in by the Colgate Brethren of a neighboring town. The reader loses sight of all the brothers and sisters except Tamar, who is a year or so younger than Susan. Tamar, the opposite of Susan in temperament, scoffs at Susan's "visions."

Eventually, Susan goes to work for Mus' Firrell, a follower of Hur Colgate, in whose home Hur Colgate spent his final years. The room in which Hur Colgate died is kept as a shrine by the Firrells. While at the Firrells, Susan meets and marries Dan Strudwick, a man who loves her completely, so much that he takes over the ordinary household tasks of a woman in order to leave his wife free to preach to the brethren. Susan loves him, also, but Strudwick dies accidentally, soon after the death of their child.

Forced to earn her living, for her preaching brings her little money, Susan accepts a position as housekeeper to Mus' Gardner, an old, well to do farmer. The old man comes to depend on her, and the life satisfies Susan. It allows her to manage a household and to preach at the same time. By this time, she has built up a reputation as preacher, and she travels to various congregations of the Colgate Brethren.

On one of these preaching missions, Susan meets Charles

Clarabut. He is of the gentry, but he has never made much of a living. Instead he lives well on the largesse of his friends. Mutually attracted, they marry, after Susan has precipitously left Mus' Gardner to join Clarabut in London. Susan, forced to live in London and forced to stop her preaching, realizes that both she and Clarabut have been disappointed in each other: Susan because she cannot sustain Clarabut's man about town way of life, and Clarabut because Susan has been cut off from the inheritance he expected her to receive from Mus' Gardner. Susan leaves Clarabut after a severe quarrel. She wanders around looking for lodging, is robbed, is befriended by two women, and is eventually taken by the women to a public house. The wife of the landlord is her sister Tamar.

At Tamar's, she encounters David Pell, a man she had known in her childhood. David has become wealthy and fanatically religious. He falls in love with Susan, and attracted by what his wealth could do to help her found her own community of Colgate Brethren, Susan encourages him. She reads in a newspaper report that her husband, Clarabut, has been drowned at sea. Susan and David are married. The plans are set for buying a large farm to settle the religious followers of David, a straggling band called "The Poor Christians." These poor families have been supported by David and will now form the nucleus of a congregation which Susan plans to lead in the same way as Hur Colgate led his followers.

Just as the scene is set for her first preaching to her new congregation, Susan receives a letter from Clarabut. This tells her that he is still alive and that he knows that she has remarried. She is, therefore, a bigamist. She is also living in "sin," which would horrify her congregation and her husband if they knew. She tears up the letter and refuses to tell anyone of her situation, secure in the knowledge that Clarabut will not reveal it to anyone else. As the novel ends, she enters her church and prepares to open the Scriptures.

IV   *The Chosen of God*

Susan Spray learns, at a very early age, that the manipulation of other peoples' naive belief in God can be used to great advantage. She also learns, from her parents, that she is a "pretty little girl, small-boned and graceful, quite an elegant little lady compared with the roundabout red-faced children of the neighbors." Her mother calls her "My Lady" and pretends that she is "very grand."[25] Thus set apart from others, Susan convinces herself at a tender age that she is, indeed, unlike others. Added to her sense of importance is a vivid imagination based on the stories in the Bible. The biblical world takes on the nature of reality for her.

Her vivid imagination forces her into her first "vision." Because God's voice is described in the Bible as being like thunder, she convinces herself that the thunder is His voice. She even convinces herself that she sees Him. Her fear overpowers the fear of a beating from her parents. The fear of God and the fear of her parents, plus the fear of the thunderstorm itself, seem "to become one in a terrible trinity," so that she doesn't know which she fears more—"her father, the storm, or God" (11).

This "terrible trinity" might be seen to symbolize the three main motivating principles of her life. Her father (authoritative approval or disapproval) becomes the measure by which she judges her success in life—the acceptance, the renown given to her by others. The storm might symbolize the vicissitudes of life which buffet her and which need to be tamed (and from which she must run to God) so that life may be comfortable and easy. God might symbolize the strength, the power, she needs to carry out her tasks, the rationalization for her headstrong challenge to the elders of her church. As Reuben Backfield uses Boarzell and Edward Monypenny uses Tamarisk Town, Susan Spray uses God to justify her actions. In this, she reveals herself as the most evil of the three, for she fails to see herself as the hypocrite she is. Instead, she poses as spiritual leader, supposedly to feed her flock, but in reality to feed her ego.

Susan's hypocrisy shows itself first when she tells the story of her "vision" to save herself a beating. Only the mocking face of her mother shows her that she is not completely believed at home, and only Springett, one of the Colgate Brethren exposes to her her "inmost self," and she wonders how he knew that " 'maybe she wanted a word from the Lord to send her home out of the racket and save her a beating.' " But she knows that if the brethren disbelieved her, "she would disbelieve herself—and she had seen the Lord—she had! she had!" (17). Throughout her life she continues to need this confirmation from others, an indication that she lacks security in her own beliefs.

Her schooling, a study of the Bible only, reaffirms her vision of
the world and reaffirms her belief that she is set apart, for most
of the Colgate children get no chance at learning to read.
Springett's contention that the brethren are " 'a poor set of
sheep, asking to be led astray by somebody . . . and gotten a
babe to do it' " is born out by their willingness to believe Susan's
revelations. And their acceptance of Susan becomes stronger
when Springett is found dead in a marl pit after a night of
drinking. They are convinced that "the Lord had surely set His
seal on Susan Spray by thus visiting with destruction the only one
of them who had doubted her word" (22). Thus begins Susan's
conviction that she is protected by God, as one of His chosen.

She feels the presence of God throughout her life. Sent out to
steal a turnip root at the age of ten, she "seemed to become a
fellow of the grass and nettles and hedges, sharing their
adornment of mist and dew, and suddenly she felt a deep
contentment rising in her heart. . . . Surely now when the world
was empty and washed like this, the Lord must walk in it, as He
used to walk in Eden long ago" (29). As she sees the sun rise
suddenly out of the mist, she convinces herself that it is a sign:
God in the Burning Bush.

Her conviction that God is near gives her great confidence in
Him. She knows, after the death of her mother, that the "Lord
God would not let her want" (38). But she also knows that she
must struggle if she is not to be caught up in the lot of women,
which is marriage, childbearing, and service at home to others.
Rejecting the usual lot of women, she dreams of herself as a great
prophet, and she sees "a picture of herself writing . . . another
Book of the Bible—the Book of Susan . . . 'The burden of
Pickdick, which Susan the prophet did see' " (52).

Her confidence in God, her conviction that the world of the
Bible is "very close and clear, a luminous world shining upon the
concrete trials and joys of this" (20), and her consideration of
herself as one of God's chosen cause her to see herself as Moses
leading her people to the Promised Land, for "like many
visionaries," she is "able to accept remarkable discrepancies
between her dream and its fulfillment" (56).

The impetus to make herself into a preacher stems from two
sources. One source is her conviction that only by throwing off
the yoke of women will she be able to attain some measure of
freedom; the other is her conviction that she is a person apart,

better in some way than her fellow creatures. She enjoys some measure of freedom, for her position as reader of the Bible to the Colgate Brethren makes her a ruler in this little world. Her own actions resemble those of boys as well as of girls, for the outside farm work is always her preference over the kitchen work usually assigned to girls. She vows that she never will be a man's wife, for her picture of a wife is a picture of a family drudge. One obstacle standing in the way of the freedom she hopes to achieve is her sister Tamar, for Tamar represents a part of herself.

She judges Tamar, even though she ordinarily does not judge others. And her judgment of Tamar includes herself. Tamar's desire to be comfortable, her complete femaleness, her contentment with the lot of women—all cause Susan to treat her with contempt, although Tamar sometimes seems "just another part of herself, pulling her a different way from the way her real self wanted to go" (80).

Susan's struggle to make herself into a seer and preacher must override the impulses she feels deep inside her, the side represented by Tamar. One of these impulses concerns the hard, but satisfying, farm work she does at Mus' Firrells. The work satisfies a deep longing in her, and as she walks alone in the quiet of the evening, she wonders if the peace she feels has its basis in religion. One part of her feels it has, but yet "it seemed remote from the restless, glamourous urge that once had driven her soul to and fro, and which had never seemed apart from life, as this mystic moment here. . . . Religion had never given her this deep peace, this quiet. . . . Nor had it ever given her this sense of her own littleness, and even less this sweet content and rest in her own littleness" (92).

At Mus' Firrell's, then, her struggling better self attempts to assert itself. Before this, religion to her had always been an ego-satisfying activity. But here she forgets "holy things, turning to things of earth" (97). The power she had heretofore experienced in holding a congregation spellbound with her preaching transforms itself into her work, as "the wheat in her hands . . . she pressed and bound with a sense of usefulness and power" (98). And Tamar adds to her confusion, for she shows her that her once-sought plans for teaching the Bible are impossible. Then Susan "would hate Tamar for being half herself and yet so unlike herself. It was as if in a manner she was bound to Tamar's low expectations" (93).

Like Reuben Backfield and Edward Monypenny, Susan Spray also is driven in opposite directions by an inherent sense of what is right but also by a stronger need to satisfy an inflated ego. She feels the satisfaction of her work on the land, which gives her peace. She also feels the pull, in the opposite direction, of her preaching, which gives her a powerful ego satisfaction. And her work on the land lessens her thoughts about religion. The natural beauties of sky and meadow provide her with a sense of wonder at their ability to bring her contentment, instead of providing thoughts about their Creator. "Oh, fallen prophet! She who had seen the Lord, now slept in sermon-time, she who had brought Israel out of Egypt and had heard the bells of Jerusalem ringing, now tumbled into bed half asleep without saying her prayers" (96-97).

Thus, physical labor on Mus' Firrell's farm satisfies her so much that she can forego her preaching. But as a woman, she cannot deny that side of herself which Tamar exemplifies fully. She feels she lacks the love that her sister so easily finds, yet she does not really want it. "The common destiny of woman still appeared to her as an infinite humiliation. She would have liked to escape. . . . Yet what other choice had she? The vague ambitions that had once stirred her were gone. . . . they seemed to her mad and hopeless. She would never be a great prophet or teacher. Tamar had shown her that. Ah, Tamar . . . it would be good to meet her on her own ground and beat her there" (101).

Subconsciously, Susan wishes to be Tamar. Hindered by her inability to reconcile Tamar's life with her own imbedded ideas of good and evil, Susan represses the side of her that is Tamar. Her only recourse, then, is to turn her envy of Tamar into Tamar's envy of her.

Because the literal belief in the sainthood of Hur Colgate is one of the forces which sustain her, she prays to him, putting her predicament into words: "When I read the Book it seems all nonsense to me, and Satan puts all manner of mocking notions into me. I don't seem to care about religion any more, and yet I don't seem to care for nothing else" (105). Susan's dilemma stems from her belief in a religion of her own making, while at the same time she knows that the religion she has made does not exist. She longs for what is not—a religion and a world made to her specifications, a world in which she leads and rules, powerful but also beloved.

Her dilemma solves itself as she stands alone in a great meadow. She knows that the embrace she had just enjoyed from the farmhand Gutsell is shameful, because it is a "false rest." She seems to hear a voice which is not really a voice but "a great surge of knowledge moving in her heart, knowledge which was love, that sighed and burned in her heart like love, the knowledge that she was Saved" (111). This conviction of her salvation gives her the impetus to continue her rebellion against accepting her place in society as a woman. She tells Strudwick that "'a woman can live alone as well as a man—and better. . . . I feel I could live a man's life—alone like a man. . . . I could live my own life my own way, just as a man does'" (116). It is her attempt to convince herself. The means to her desired end will be preaching the gospel.

Her trouble stems not only from the necessity of overturning conventional behavior, but also from her lingering doubts about her calling. Her better self, hidden deep in her consciousness, asserts itself to make her wonder with "a fear that was almost knowledge" whether her public preaching might cause her to lose her "deep heart's content" (120). Her ambition to become a teacher now becomes a threat to her peace. "A voice said 'Get up'; another said 'Sit still.' 'Get up and preach—show them what you can do, and one day you'll be a great preacher and forget the curse of being a woman'—'Sit still, and your joy no man taketh from you. Remember that a woman once bore the Son of God'" (120).

But the call to her ego when she contemplates the power that preaching will give her, particularly over Tamar, forces her to still the voice which tells her to "sit still." This power, together with her sense of self, soars as she reaps the praise and respect which feed her vanity. This vanity "had none of that personal, physical element which is so big a part of the vanity of most women; it fed entirely on her works, on her position with regard to other folk, and now on this gift of preaching with which she dazzled her neighbors" (130).

Only because Strudwick becomes a model husband for her can she have the best of both worlds—as a wife and as a preacher. Actually, he loves her for her superiority over him. As for her, the more she can show herself his superior, the more she loves him, for "she could never have loved the governing man of the marriage service" (136).

This happy state of affairs, a blending of career and wifehood, ends for Susan Spray, as does Joanna Godden's happy state of affairs, with the death of her husband. Sheila Kaye-Smith seems to provide a happy solution to the problem of a woman attempting to reach maturity—the love of a noncompetitive man—but she also indicates that this solution will be destroyed by fate or by the nature of things.

Susan has now received two severe blows which test her belief in herself as one of God's chosen—the death of her son and the death of Strudwick. Making the matter worse, how can she reconcile God's loving care of her with the death of her son and the thriving of Tamar's bastard son? Her little son had been more precious to her than the marriage which produced him. She sinks, in her estimation, to the depth in which she would be willing to change places with Tamar, could she but have her son.

When asked to preach, she hears again "that same protesting whisper in her heart. But this time it was even more quickly silenced" (153). And her hurt over the loss of her son lashes out at Tamar, and in lashing out at Tamar, it is lashing out at the God Susan Spray has created. "Tamar had done this to mock her. . . her pursed plum of mouth was saying 'Look how much better my wickedness has done than your goodness. You should ought to have been wicked like me'" (158).

Her refusal to receive Tamar's son as a Colgate Brethren stems from her envy of her and from her need to rationalize her God's action. If she is not God's chosen one,

why should her enemies all through her life have been so signally and powerfully overthrown? The very circumstances which had been designed by them for her humiliation had turned instead to her credit. She thought of Springett the smith at Copthorne, who had doubted her first vision, and had come to a bad end, dying like a dog. . . . And now Tamar, who had sought to mock her, to glory over her with her living child—all that Tamar had done had been to seal her triumph in the congregation and extend her fame to unimagined fields outside it. (163-64)

Unable to find happiness as Tamar has, unable to satisfy the side of her that is Tamar, Susan has no recourse but to feed her vanity. She has always felt superior to those to whom she preached, but now she must add the superiority of possessions. When she receives her first gold coin for her preaching, she vows to have a bonnet as fine as any worn by the ladies to whom she preaches the vanity of worldly possessions. Her inflated ego soars so high that in her dream she has the sensation of being mistress of the world, "saying triumphantly 'I am my own—I am my own' " (166).

Also, she constantly feels the need to justify to herself the God she has created out of her ignorance and her ego. She justifies Strudwick's death by telling herself that God wants her to lean on herself, but she has no justification for the fact that Tamar, who had neither served the Lord nor preached, has a happy life with her child and her lover while she has neither child nor husband. "It would almost seem as if the divine justice were at fault. Yet Susan would not doubt the Lord" (175). And the reason she dare not doubt is that "to have questioned His providence or doubted His power would somehow have humbled her own soul. For her sake He must be justified" (175). Having set herself up as God's chosen one, she cannot allow her belief in herself as "chosen" to be destroyed. It is the source of her ego satisfaction.

For a similar reason, her imagination transforms the very mundane facts of her existence into biblical events of great magnitude: "He had brought her wonderfully and miraculously out of Surrey, out of the land of Egypt, He had preserved her when the rest of her folk were scattered, He had shared with her the terrible triumph into Jerusalem, into the gates of Horsham, He had magnified her in the congregations and lifted up her head among the Brethren" (176). It must be for some mysterious purpose of His own that he had "taken from her her child, her hope and her Savior." In her mind, the child represented Christ himself—and of course that would make her the Mother of Christ. Now "He had taken her husband, and all her comfort and honour and independence. So Susan trusted in God" (176).

Refusing to look at herself as one of God's humble creatures, one on a level with all others, Susan Spray continually feeds her own monstrous ego by struggling to reach the pinnacle it sets up. Rationalization takes the place of reason. Although this rationalization clouds reality for her, it also provides the courage for her to attempt a career unheard of for a woman of her time.

Through her rationalization, Susan believes in herself again.

And there is an added reward. She has experienced the humanizing effect of personal sorrow, for "her unicorn had become a common ass which the people of the Forest could like and understand. . . . sorrow had hobbled her, made her stay with the flock" (180). As she humanizes her message, she receives unexpected rewards. She becomes more sought after than ever. As has been her experience throughout her life, the renown goes to her head, and she sees herself "a mighty preacher, known throughout the world, her womanhood trodden down and forgotten" (180).

Thus Susan's problem at this time is twofold; she must struggle to satisfy the ego which has convinced her that she is a being set apart, and she must transcend her sex. If she accepts the offer to be leader of the congregation at Brighton, she will be "free and independent . . . as good as a minister, as good as a man . . . escaped forever from the common lot of women" (193). She finds the answer to her inward insecurities by telling herself that the Holy Ghost gives her her words in the pulpit. Her own imagination provides the fuel for lighting up the words of the Bible to make them applicable to herself.

She equates her own fame with the glory of God. The more the congregation trembles at her words, the more renown she gains. The humanizing effect of sorrow on her sermons becomes lost in this need for renown which she rationalizes as a need to glorify God. This unbeatable combination—Susan Spray's renown and God's glory—must be ever spread wider and wider. She must found a new congregation. "Hur Colgate had given them two gates, but the third gate was the Gospel of Susan Strudwick—the Gate of Birth and the Gate of Death and the Gate of the Temple. She kept the Gate of the Temple . . . she saw herself guarding it as the angel with the fiery sword" (192). She will be as the Apostle Paul, preaching to various congregations and drawing them into her vision. And Tamar will be full of envy at the sight of her as prophet of this new dispensation—she hopes.

But she is betrayed by her need for physical love. She knows very well that love for Clarabut is leading her into wantonness. She is becoming more and more like Tamar. The Tamar side of her struggles for ascendancy. The conflict between her love for Clarabut and her love for her ministry tears her apart, and her preaching becomes "tortured, consumed." The real struggle lies between her desires to transcend both the lot of common people and the lot of women by gaining fame and fortune, and the Tamar side of her, which desires a husband and family. The normal need for expressions of love, in giving and taking, exposes her to herself. Unable to reconcile what she preaches and what she feels, she begins to see herself as the humbug Clarabut affectionately calls her, for "she had chosen the gospel—and she did not believe in it any more" (250).

Susan Spray goes through her own particular Gethsemane, seeing reality for the first time. She knows that the things she has been telling herself had happened to her had not really happened at all. She knows that her preaching begins to be a justification of herself rather than a proclamation of the Lord's message. She no longer relies on her own image of God to define her. Now it is Clarabut who defines her. The "only part of her present life that seemed real was Clarabut. It was the sight of him sitting there opposite her, talking and eating, which told her who she was" (263). She faces herself and her own self-deception, knowing that "she was a humbug—lying to herself about gates and visions and temples, which had never been, yet which somehow she could not bear to have lost" (270).

She realizes more. She knows now that her choice of Clarabut over her preaching was not the time she "betrayed her soul," but it was rather when she "stood up before them all in Hendall's barn and told them the secret of what had happened to her in the field, choosing to preach instead of to pray, to be Paul of Tarsus instead of Mary of Bethany. It was then, and not at any later choice that the Scriptures had condemned her to suffer vanity even as the fool" (285). The prayers could have, and indeed did, come when she stood alone in the fields, with God's creation bringing peace into her heart. But she needed to do, rather than to be, and she realizes it.

Yet, she cannot take the final step into maturity; she cannot give up the lies on which she has built not only her life, but her own existence. Her visions "may not have happened, but they're true" (290). Susan Spray builds her reality on a false premise. She is set apart, chosen of God. The visions, therefore, are true, even though she did not see them. The apparent contradiction does not trouble her. Her need to reaffirm herself remains too great.

Her fall from the grace almost within her grasp is startling. She can tell David Pell, "I'm Gospel and you're Gold and we're both

Glorious. . . . Glory for me and Glory for you" (339). The glory of the Lord has been subsumed in the glory of His creatures. She thinks of herself as pope of the poor christians, as she decides their fate. She sees David's wealth as God's special providence. "All these years the Lord had been making David Pell rich, so that at the appointed time he could succour and establish Susan Spray" (340). Although she enjoys scaring her congregations with visions of hell because of their sinfulness, in her eyes there is only one sin, "doubting her word" (345).

The fall is complete. She alone stands as the author of truth, infallible, protected by God's providence, chosen of God. She stifles the doubts which cause her, at times, to feel a lack of virtue in herself. Only by marrying David Pell, who will follow her, rather than she him, will she be able to continue to escape the common lot of women. She will "have the comforts of a husband and a home without any of the drawbacks." Her marriage to David will "proclaim forever her triumph over the common lot of women" (366).

With her marriage to David, Susan Spray feels that she has what she has always wanted: "enough work, much preaching and a little love" (378). Because she has what she has always wanted within her grasp, she knows that nothing, not even the hypocrisy of the life she will be forced to live as a bigamist, will shake her from her chosen path. Clarabut will never be able to move her aside. He "did not know who fought for Susan Spray" (384).

Thus, with a headdress "like a turban and a mitre and a crown and a halo . . . erect and proud, full of her own triumph and the triumph of the Church of Jehovah-Jireh" (385), she moves solemnly to the desk which holds the Scriptures and opens the Book. She has come full circle, having met the Trinity of her fears and triumphed over it. The authority, symbolized by the mitre and crown, has passed from her father and from the men in her life to her. She has triumphed over all, for all look up to her as authority. The halo symbolizes her loss of fear of God, for she is God's chosen, and He would not let anything happen to her. She is saved. The triumph symbolizes her triumph over the material needs of life, for as David's wife, she will never want for material comforts.

The trinity of her fears, experienced long ago when she was a child of six, has been abolished through the struggle which, propelled by her ego, ends with her conviction that she is authority; she is, in a sense, God. She will experience a life of comfort and ease while enjoying the homage of her congregation. Her struggle has succeeded. She has, indeed, thrown off the ordinary yoke of women, and in doing so, she has triumphed over Tamar who, an ordinary wife, must remain subject to her husband.

Susan Spray's story is, on the surface, a story of the struggle of a woman to break out of the mold society has set for her. On this level, it reveals the thoughts and feelings of an ambitious young woman attempting to make herself into a complete human being. But on a deeper level, the story speaks to all who, lacking the wisdom to accept themselves as intrinsically worthy and equal to their sisters and brothers in humanity, compete for a valid place in the universe.

Susan's competition is primarily her sister Tamar. But Tamar represents one part of herself. In triumphing over Tamar by becoming another Hur Colgate, she has triumphed over that part of herself which, properly blended into her being, would have made her into a more mature person in a proper measure of intellect, emotion, and will. By denying those qualities of human warmth and clarity of vision which are Tamar's, Susan Spray ends up with all of the wantonness she sees in Tamar and none of Tamar's saving grace.

Like Reuben Backfield, Susan Spray seems contented with the person she has made herself into and with the life she has made for that person. Convinced that she has gained her goal, she remains serene in the face of her knowledge that she is the complete opposite of what her husband and her congregation think her to be. Her conviction, like Backfield's, that she alone is right, brings her comfort. There is no hint that she progresses further.

Of all Sheila Kaye-Smith's protagonists who struggle for selfhood through ambition, Susan Spray stands as the most morally deficient, if morality is seen as the ability to act honestly toward others. However, Sheila Kaye-Smith pronounces no judgment on her or on any of the others. Subjectively speaking, one can find that Susan Spray has used her talents for her own gain. Objectively speaking, one finds that she has prostituted these talents to the end that she becomes the greatest hypocrite of all—a humbug, as, in more lucid moments, she characterizes herself.

On another level, the stories of Joanna Godden and Susan Spray represent their author's apparent conviction that a woman's struggle is twofold. Not only must she gain, through her actions, her own being, but she must also overcome all the obstacles put in her way by manmade conventions. When Joanna Godden accepts these conventions and works within them, she succeeds in becoming strong and, in a measure, content. When Susan Spray refuses to accept them, she strays beyond the realm of morality and ends as a hypocrite.

Sheila Kaye-Smith assigns no blame to any of her characters. One is free, then, to assign the responsibility for the monstrous hypocrisy of Susan Spray to a society which is so harsh and cruel that her only recourse is to meet it with the same harshness and cruelty, since she cannot accept her place as a woman in it. For her, a little knowledge is indeed a dangerous thing, and the self-blinding necessary to satisfy her ego leads, as it does in the case of Backfield and Monypenny, not to wisdom but to the tragedy (in the Judao-Christian point of view, at least) of failure to love God and neighbor.

CHAPTER 4

Later Life and Later Novels

S HEILA Kaye-Smith wrote *Sussex Gorse* during World War I.
Even though "for about a week before and a week after war
was declared . . . most writers imagined their work was done
for . . . the war seemed to give an urge to literature, especially
to the more sensitive and imaginative kinds."[1] Although Miss
Kaye-Smith confesses that she "personally. . .felt guilty till the
end of the war,"[2] she never felt herself absorbed in, or distracted
by, the war, even though she did a certain amount of work,
making swabs and bandages and selling doughnuts in a canteen.
But she enjoyed the writing of *Sussex Gorse*, for she saw it as an
escape from the unhappiness around her.

Sussex Gorse brought its author critical and popular acclaim,
and she remembers the "few weeks following the publication of
Sussex Gorse as some of the happiest" of her life.[3] But the
"complex of war runs to herds and crowds," and she was drawn
to London, finding her heart "not in the country as it used to be."
Her imagination was "busy with a town," and thus the idea for
Tamarisk Town was born. But she found that she could not finish
the novel, and she put it aside to write *The Challenge to Sirius*
and *Little England*.[4]

I   The Challenge to Sirius; Little England

The Challenge to Sirius, was, for its author, "a novel of
escape."[5] It relieved "that part" of her "which sought not escape
but expression." She wrote about the Civil War, therefore, but it
was her way of writing about the war at hand.[6] At this time, also,
her dormant religious sense stirred, and she interested herself in
Anglo-Catholicism, feeling "at home" while participating in a
"luxurious High Mass" at St. Alban's. Here she felt "was the right
atmosphere for religion—warm, living, splendid, slightly exotic."

86   SHEILA KAYE-SMITH

Feeling that "something very deep" in her heart "was stirred, as
it had not been stirred in the Catholic church," she "lifted up"
her eyes and "looked towards home."⁷

The Challenge to Sirius did not receive the acclaim afforded
Sussex Gorse. Its author feels that it is overburdened by scenery
and philosophy. The personal struggles expressed in it represent
her own at the time, as she felt both remote from God and on her
way back to Him.⁸ Although her agent felt that she had offended
the Church of Rome in the novel, she pointed out to him that her
study was really a sympathetic one, as she had given "Romanism
at its worst the advantage over Anglicanism at its best." But her
own inner turmoil and her leanings towards Catholicism must
have been perceived by at least one perceptive reader, for
"actually all that happened was that a Jesuit priest, reading it
down in Sussex," marked her "as one who should and possibly
would join the Catholic Church." It was this same priest who
later received her into the Roman Catholic church.⁹

The other novel written during World War I concerns the war
directly. Sheila Kaye-Smith now found herself able to deal with
it outright and not under the guise she had invented in *The
Challenge to Sirius.* She felt that the public did not sufficiently
appreciate this book on its publication. The characters in it
appear as little people, not bigger than life as in her previous
novels. But the war ended, and people wished to forget it and,
along with it, war stories. Despite the author's claims for it, *Little
England* has neither the interesting characters nor the psychological depth of her other novels.

II   *Return to Religion*

The end of the war brought Miss Kaye-Smith a new life, and
this reflected her growing interest in Anglo-Catholicism. She
writes that she spent "twelve years as a sort of synthetic Catholic
in the Church of England," being put off by the "outward
severity of Catholicism."¹⁰ Surprisingly to her, it was her
happiness at this time that revealed to her her need of religion.¹¹
She therefore made her first confession in the Church of
England in the winter of 1918.

She feels that most of what critics consider her best work was
accomplished after her return to religion. *Tamarisk Town*
(1919),¹² *Green Apple Harvest* (1920), and *Joanna Godden*

(1922) followed this return. *The End of the House of Alard* (1923) is ordinarily considered to be her first "Anglo-Catholic" story, while *Tamarisk Town* is the first to sell more than a thousand copies. It sold three thousand. *Green Apple Harvest* remains what she considers her best book. She writes, "in this I have the support of no less an authority than George Moore." She feels, also, that in this book she has placed the characters "in that middle light between realism and romance which is the best to read human nature by." She admits, though, that while some of the reviews were good, some were not.[13]

III   Joanna Godden; The End of the House of Alard

Willy George, as she had nicknamed George Moore, gave Sheila Kaye-Smith the idea for *Joanna Godden* when, while walking through a farmyard, he spied a woman's name on a farm wagon. He asked her why she didn't write a book about a woman farmer. She objected that she "did not like writing about women" and had "never before made a woman [her] central character." She confessed further that she "did not want to spend six months in female company." The fact that she scarcely knew a man except her father bothered her not at all, as she wrote from imagination rather than from observation. She is similar to Emily Bronte in some respects: both wrote out of an innocence of life, with intense passion and with great imagination, and both expressed a powerful personality. Both saw, also, the somber side of personality and created male characters whose motivation seemed to arise from some dark recess of the human spirit. Although she "definitely preferred a man's society,"[14] she found herself "surprisingly at . . . ease" while writing Joanna's story, finding Joanna "with her reckless, splendid notions, her conceit and her warm heart . . . not . . . such bad company after all." Her friend Willy George did not like *Joanna Godden*. He felt that her creator had made Joanna "too much of a virago."[15]

Joanna Godden became so much of a success that her readers never let her forget it. Sheila Kaye-Smith found it trying that she had to "hear *Joanna Godden* sighed over as the last novel [she] wrote before religion spoilt [her] as a novelist." She feels that *Joanna Godden* contains, in reality, various clues as to her religious convictions. It annoyed her that the contrast between

Joanna Godden and the first novel after her conversion to Anglo-Catholicism, *The End of the House of Alard*, was "commonly put down to religion" and that "according to the rather naive views of authorship held by some readers and even by some critics," she had "immediately sat down to write about" her newfound religion.[16]

For fifteen years after its publication, *Joanna Godden* was held up to her as "an example of the excellent work [she] used to do in the days before [she] became mixed up with religion." She found that "if Sussex is a label, religion is a dye and there is no getting rid of it."[17] Her comment on this point is interesting. "The public does not necessarily object to propaganda, but it likes the propaganda to propagate something it wants, like divorce, not something like Catholicism which it does not want and largely disapproves of. Criticism at once ceases to be candid, for the majority of critics so dislike the colour of one's thoughts that they refuse to look at any beauty there may be in the form that embodies it, whereas the minority whose view one is expressing can see no possible defect in that expression."[18] Actually, she feels that there is not one of her novels in which religion does not appear to some extent, except *Tamarisk Town*, in "the middle of which [she] found it."[19]

But *The End of the House of Alard* does contain her religious convictions. She admits that in it she was "definitely challenging and proclaiming, and here—speaking from a religious as well as from an artistic point of view—[her] error lay." She attributes the propagandizing of her religious views to the fact that she felt the need to justify them, to rationalize her beliefs.[20]

The death of her father at this time interrupted her writing for awhile, but the publication of *The End of the House of Alard* brought her tremendous financial success. She considered it an inferior book, and the Reverend C. C. Martindale, writing in the *Dublin Review*, calls it a "thesis."[21]

Part of the popularity of *The End of the House of Alard* rested, undoubtedly, on the fact that she had just been warmly welcomed into the Anglo-Catholic church, which had severely felt the loss of Gilbert Keith Chesterton to Rome. Her Anglo-Catholicism, therefore, was made much of, and the popularity of the novel depended, perhaps, more on its religious view than on its standing as a literary work. Sheila Kaye-Smith herself believed that the "Anglo-Catholic movement was the divinely appointed way of England's return to Catholicism." Later, when she joined the Catholic church in 1929, she mainly changed her "allegiance, due to [her] conviction that Catholicism cannot exist apart from the Church which Christ himself established on the rock of Peter." Other than that, she states, "there is no fundamental difference between what I believe and work for now and what I believed and worked for then."[22]

IV *Marriage*

Her marriage in 1924 to a clergyman, Reverend F. Penrose Fry, then Anglican rector at St. Leonards-on-Sea, brought her the necessity of living in London[23] when he was transferred there. But her imagination still fed on Sussex and Kent, and *Saints in Sussex* (a volume of poetry),[24] *Joanna Godden Married* (a volume of short stories), *Iron and Smoke, The Village Doctor,* and *Shepherds in Sackcloth* were all written in London.

Soon after her marriage, both her sister and her mother died, leaving her bereft not only of them, but also of the home she used to visit in St. Leonards. Her sister has been immortalized as the Moira in *The Children's Summer* and *Selina (Selina Is Older).*[25] As a clergyman's wife, the author found as much time for writing as she had before, as the couple had income other than that of a clergyman's salary. She felt herself to be fortunate, as she writes: "I know of nothing more destructive to the literary impulse than scrubbing and cooking."[26]

The novels written in London did not enjoy as much critical acclaim or as many sales as her previous books. Sheila Kaye-Smith attributes this to the fact that she could not revive her interest in Joanna Godden to make the continuation of her story a success;[27] that *Iron and Smoke* suffered too much from its author's " 'thinking' "; and that *The Village Doctor* was "altogether too slight and conventional a story."[28]

At this time, Sheila Kaye-Smith and her husband lived in South Kensington, both uneasy in their Anglo-Catholicism. She had always believed that Anglo-Catholicism would eventually become Roman Catholicism and had worked toward that end. She became as "Catholic" as the Church of England would allow. To leave the Church of England seemed cowardly to her, like giving up the fight; yet the Roman Catholic church drew her thoughts and practices.

To allay some of this uneasiness, Sheila Kaye-Smith and her clergyman husband took a cruise to Italy in September of 1928. They expected that the sight of religion, as practiced there, would cure them of their leanings toward Rome. Instead, they found that the cathedrals were "really providing religion, and providing it not only for the pious few, but for many, for the workers, for that man in the street to whom Anglicanism gives such a raw deal." As they left, they felt that they knew that that was the place they really belonged.[29]

Shepherds in Sackcloth is the last novel written before Miss Kaye-Smith's conversion to Roman Catholicism. For her, it is the story of a "growing disillusion." She feels that there is "no propaganda in the story" except her wish to make the old parson and his wife "better understood."[30]

She is "glad that [her] last novel as an Anglican should have been a tribute to two of the worthiest and most misunderstood members of the community—the English clergyman and his wife."[31] *Shepherds in Sackcloth* represents an entirely sympathetic picture of a poor clergyman. Parson Carpenter in *The View from the Parsonage* is not quite as sympathetic a character as is Mr. Bennet, the shepherd in sackcloth. Parson Carpenter's absence of sackcloth is readily apparent.

V   *Conversion to Roman Catholicism*

The conversion to Catholicism for both Sheila Kaye-Smith and her husband represented less of a change for them in leaving their religion than it did for them in leaving the clerical life, for both had been Catholic in their convictions. They merely changed their "allegiance."[32] They continued religious work from the little farm they had purchased in Sussex, "Little Doucegrove." The author writes

it was a work that quite definitely seemed given us to do; we should never have thought of choosing it, or even—in those early days—have guessed that it could be chosen. As for many years there was no resident priest, it meant more "parish work" than I, certainly, have ever done in my life. To visit the sick, round up the backsliders, teach the children, care for the sanctuary, take the collections, "answer the Mass," are all of them things I should never have dreamed of doing in my husband's parishes. Indeed, I have never felt more of a clergyman's wife than since I ceased to be one.[33]

The fact that the couple enjoyed financial independence gave them the freedom to answer the call of their desire. In addition to the duties described above, Sheila Kaye-Smith also helped to make Little Doucegrove liveable, and she continued her writing. She wrote, here, *Susan Spray*, which was attacked as being " 'Jesuitical propaganda' " and an "exposure of the evils of Protestantism and an attack on women preachers." She insists that she intended neither.[34]

In the house in which Father Martindale first read *The Challenge to Sirius*, he instructed the couple in the Catholic religion. They gave up Anglo-Catholicism, but they "parted friends."[35] In an Epilogue to *Three Ways Home*, Miss Kaye-Smith makes an interesting parallel between Catholicism and marriage.

Just as the evidence of a happy marriage does not lie in the couple's exclamation of rapture or the embraces they give each other—especially in public—so in a happy Catholicism there are fewer shouts of joy, more acts of penitence, less outward bustle and protestation, more turning away of the soul to her own quiet home. That is why most converts have so little to say about themselves after joining the Church. Their history is like the history of a happily married pair—not half so interesting as if it had not been half so happy.[36]

And happy she apparently was, both in her conversion and in her marriage. Mass was said at Little Doucegrove in December of 1930, the first time Mass had been said, publicly, in that neighborhood since the Reformation. However, a local tradition to the effect that it was said secretly near there—a tradition born out by a local place name "Superstition Corner"—gave Sheila Kaye-Smith the basis for the first of her two Catholic novels, *Superstition Corner*. This novel concerns the banishment of the Mass in 1559, and it gives a historical perspective on the persecution of the Catholic religion from that time. It concerns also the history of the Alards and the Douces, which history ends with *The End of the House of Alard. Superstition Corner* covers the entire period of the persecution, Miss Kaye-Smith ended it and wrote *Gallybird* as a sequel. This carried the history into the seventeenth century. Neither of these two "Catholic" novels pleased their author, and she felt that there was no longer any connection between herself and her work.

To attempt to find this connection again, she wrote two autobiographical novels based on her childhood, *The Children's*

Summer (1933) and *Selina Is Older* (1935), neither of which is "quite plain fact or quite pure fiction."[37] Then she wrote *Rose Deeprose* (1936), which, she feels, exhibits a "method of literary construction which could be carried further." The earlier books contain "whole episodes in chunks from life," while in *Rose Deeprose* the "particles have been better digested . . . the material is not taken out in patches but pulled out in threads which are woven together unrecognizable into a new stuff." She further believes that she should never again "write from the secret storehouse" of her mind, but rather must seek the fusion of both internal and external.[38]

However, Sheila Kaye-Smith's assessment of *Rose Deeprose* is not the assessment of the present writer, nor is it, apparently, the assessment of most of her critics. Although it is entertaining, as are all of her novels, it does not reach the high level of achievement of the novels selected for analysis in this study.

VI   Life at Doucegrove

The author enjoyed a happy life at Little Doucegrove. She particularly liked the habit of her husband, Penrose, of bringing her tea early in the morning, although they breakfasted together at nine. When she had her early tea, she "could lie and think how truly happy she was, living in the country; and plan how she would write that day's piece of her current book."[39]

Her books followed in rapid succession. Although she appeared in England and in America, occasionally, as a speaker, her life was primarily that of a "writing" writer, a thorough professional. She devoted ten of fourteen lines in *Who's Who* to a "straightforward listing of her books."[40]

She kept writing through the Battle of Britain, "plugging her ears to keep out the murderous din." She had given money and land for a Catholic Church to be built near her home in 1935, dedicating it to St. Theresa of Lisieux.[41] Here she could enjoy those religious duties which were central to her life.

In a review of *Speaking of Jane Austen* (which Miss Kaye-Smith wrote with G.B. Stern), the reviewer writes that "Miss Kaye-Smith is sober, well-informed. . . . Nowhere are Jane Austen, her life and her art more firmly placed in their proper historical and social perspective, and nowhere has her 'insensitiveness' to the outer life of her time (much of it so brutal and so bloody) been better explained than in the unpretentious talk entitled 'All the New Poems and States of the Nation.' "[42] But a reference to and an understanding of Miss Kaye-Smith's state of mind during World War II might see in this "insensitiveness" a sensitivity too deep to face the horrors of World War II, just as she could not face the horrors of World War I.

Sheila Kaye-Smith died at her home on January 14, 1956. She left a heritage of more than thirty novels, written over a span of more than four decades. She also left several volumes of poetry. In addition, she left three autobiographical works: *Three Ways Home* (1937), *Kitchen Fugue* (1945), and *All the Books of My Life* (1956), as well as an appraisal of the author's works in *John Galsworthy* (1916) and *Samuel Richardson* (1911). Her other works include a book of religious essays, *The Mirror of the Months* (1925), and with G.B. Stern, *Speaking of Jane Austen* and *More Speaking of Jane Austen*.

In the beginning of *Kitchen Fugue*, Sheila Kaye-Smith writes: "Some years ago I was chidden by a reviewer for writing my religious autobiography without once mentioning either Hitler or Mussolini. I have not been able to keep the former entirely out of this, but I state in advance that I do not propose to give as much space to his activities as to my own."[43] Throughout her writing career, except for *Little England*, Sheila Kaye-Smith kept outside events pretty well out of her works. Her religious conversions, of course, apparently had some effect on her writing, but because they did not really change her beliefs, there was no need for her to emphasize any change in ideas. Her writing, based on intuition, observation, and imagination, transcends time and place, so that she can feel herself as much at home in sixteenth century England as in the twentieth century, or even in Yucatan, which she uses as locale in *The Challenge to Sirius*, even though she has never been there.

Her life, therefore, might be summed up in the comment of her friend G.B. Stern, who remarks that "three ways home were clearly marked out for her: writing, the country, and her religion, and she followed them with a child's directness."[44] The importance of the countryside of Sussex has already been indicated in the analysis of the foregoing novels. The importance of religion as well as her theological views can be seen in *The End of the House of Alard* and in her last published novel, *The View from the Parsonage*.

CHAPTER 5

Religion and Family

ALTHOUGH, as pointed out above, Sheila Kaye-Smith believed to be naive the view of those readers and critics of *The End of the House of Alard* who felt she had, in this novel "immediately sat down to write" about Anglo-Catholicism after her conversion, certainly her preoccupation with her chosen religion forms a large part of the book. But the novel contains much more than an apologia for her faith; it reveals that faith in the lives of the characters.

Criticism of *The End of the House of Alard* ranges from that of Raymond Mortimer, who indicates that "it leaves me hoping I shall never have to read another novel of the same sort,"[1] to that of A. J. Dawson, who writes that it is "with all deliberation that one applies the word genius to this writer's work, which has reached beyond the field of trained and brilliant observation to the imaginative heights which are accessible only to genius."[2] Raymond Mortimer, however, reveals a more positive assessment in admitting that Sheila Kaye-Smith's characters "behave intelligibly and have a distinct resemblance to human beings,"[3] while A. J. Dawson admits that *The End of the House of Alard* shows no advance from *Sussex Gorse, Tamarisk Town, A Challenge to Sirius, Spell Land,* and others in simple attractiveness.[4] Fletcher Allen points out that "the Church looms large in the story." He also supplies the interesting fact that "curiously enough, all the Sussex Alards now living are priests." This "now," of course, refers to the year 1924. He adds that the rector of Northiam, "the Reverend A. Frewen Aylward . . . is a descendant in direct line of the Alard who was rector of Northiam in 1595."[5]

Mary Stack expresses the opinion that "most of Sheila Kaye-Smith's characters are dominated by some emotion which colors, and frequently warps, their otherwise drab lives. . . . More often, though, this emotion seems but the expression of the great trilogy of Sussex love: love of God, love of man, and love of land. . . . Usually it is land." She further points out that "Sussex is her domain, her literary private property, as Wessex was that of Hardy," but that this is "at once an advantage and a handicap." Although her novels are "firmly rooted in the Sussex earth," which makes her "close to reality, at times the great similarity among her books suggests a literary recipe, taken out every six months, varied with an extra dash of spice, a new ingredient or two, seasoned to taste and put before the public." Too many of her novels, Miss Stack feels, "fall short of the attainments of a few."[6]

The foregoing but points out the difficulty in assessing Sheila Kaye-Smith's novels. It appears to be impossible to rate them against each other except on the purely external scale of popularity or critical acclaim. Each has its excellences; each its weaknesses.

It would be difficult to cite an author whose entire work, particularly if that work is prolific, remains on the same high level of achievement. Sheila Kaye-Smith's novels do show a similarity in theme and setting. They are informed, also, by a vision which Sheila Kaye-Smith constantly sees and delineates in her novels. But the images vary, so that the emphasis falls now on one side of personality and again on another. Although *Sussex Gorse, Tamarisk Town, and Susan Spray* all embody the theme of ambition, each novel focuses on a different aspect of personality in the protagonist through which this theme comes forth. There results, therefore, not only variety, but also a probing of various facets of human nature in action. In like manner, *The End of the House of Alard* (1923) and *The View from the Parsonage* (1954) are separated not only by three decades but also by a point of view which, although unchanging in its fundamental beliefs, looks at the same religion from two different aspects.

I   The End of the House of Alard

The story begins a few days before Christmas in the year 1918, although the reader is made aware of the roots of the Alards, which extend back to the Crusades and even before. Sir John

Alard, the squire of Conster, finds it impossible to keep up his lands, but the family lives outwardly in its accustomed luxurious manner. The lands, heavily mortgaged, require a great deal of money to remain Alard property. There are six living Alard children: Peter, George, Mary, Doris, Gervase, and Jenny. One son, Hugh, has been killed in the war.

Peter Alard has just returned from the war, heir to the Alard estate. George Alard holds the living as rector at Leasan and lives comfortably with his wife Rose. Mary is married to Julian Pembroke, while Doris has remained unmarried. Gervase and Jenny, both unmarried, are much younger than their brothers and sisters.

The novel's division consists of four parts: "Conster Manor," home of Sir John Alard, his wife, and unmarried children; "Leasan Parsonage," home of George Alard and his wife Rose; "Fourhouses," home of Ben Godfrey, whom Jenny marries; and "Starvecrow," home of Peter after his marriage. The emphasis of the story follows these homes and the people in them. Fundamentally, however, the plot revolves around Peter Alard and his romance with Stella Mount, daughter of a poor doctor.

When Peter returns from the war, he knows that he must marry a wealthy heiress if the Alard estate is to be saved, even though he is in love with Stella Mount. The love between Peter and Stella has been of several year's duration, and it is intense. But Peter gives up Stella to marry Vera, a wealthy Jewess, who brings the needed wealth to the Alard family. They live at Starvecrow, part of the Alard estate. A daughter is born to Peter and Vera, and Peter realizes that he cannot live without Stella. He fails to convince her that they should carry on an illicit love affair. Stella realizes that if she does not move away, she will not be able to withstand Peter's entreaties and will move into what she considers a sinful relationship with him. She plans, therefore, to move away with her father. Peter commits suicide.

George Alard, completely under his father's dictatorial influence, realizes that his life as a clergyman has been a failure. He compares his own life unfavorably to that of Father Luce, a High Church clergyman, whose church Stella Mount and her father attend. His brother, Gervase, also in love with Stella, joins Father Luce's church. George suffers a heart attack and, before he dies, asks that Father Luce administer the last rites to him. He receives the Last Sacrament from the hands of Father Luce.

Mary realizes that the love she once had for her husband no longer exists. She becomes friendly with Charles Smith, an older man. The friendship is misconstrued by her husband, and he sues for divorce, even though he himself is guilty of adultery. Mary wishes not to contest the suit, but Sir John Alard insists that she fight the suit and clear her name. She loses the suit and becomes disillusioned with herself and with life.

Doris remains unmarried. She is the only one who sincerely mourns the death of her father, even though he has treated her abominably throughout her life.

Jennie marries Ben Godfrey of Fourhouses, against the wishes of her family who do not wish her to marry outside of her class. She remains happy in her choice, taking on the duties of a prosperous farmer's wife. Gervase, on the death of Sir John and George, and the suicide of Peter, becomes heir to the Alard estate. However, he refuses to leave the monastery he has joined. Instead, he plans to sell the estate to provide a living for his mother and his sister.

Stella Mount, a devout Anglo-Catholic, blames herself for Peter's suicide. Gervase attempts to make her see that her action in planning to leave was the right one, but her crisis of faith drags her through misery. The story ends with the contemplated sale of the estate.

II *Love and Duty: Religion and Convention*

The End of the House of Alard contains two parallel themes: one concerns the conflict between the attempt to promulgate the traditions of the squire class and the encroachment of a lower class, and the other concerns the conflict between the Low Church of Leasan and the High Church of Vinehall. The former theme appears in the story of the attempt of the Alards to carry on their name and tradition; the latter theme appears in the story of George Alard, who finds his ministry superficial and unsatisfying. These two themes intermingle, but because the novel is divided into four distinct parts which present four different stories, analysis requires a separation, for clarity, of these two themes.

Despite the feeling of many critics that emphasis in *The End of the House of Alard* is on religion, both the title of the novel and the bulk of its story point rather toward an emphasis on the downfall of the House of Alard and its cause. The cause is twofold: first, the age old habits of squire and servant now are replaced not only by a more democratic outlook after World War I, but also by the failure of the gentry to work the land for profit. The heavy mortgages required to pay servants and to live in luxury put the estate into such debt that only the influx of new wealth can save it; second, the core of life rots before the requirement that each member of the family sacrifice himself or herself to what is best for the family. This requirement not only destroys the happiness of the person, but actually leads to the physical destruction of George, through a heart attack, and of Peter, through suicide, as well as to the spiritual destruction of Mary, through her disillusion with life because of the actions she has been forced to take. Gervase and Jenny save themselves, but they gain their freedom only by repudiating the values of pride and prestige residing in the family name.

In addition to the above evidence as to the emphasis of the story, a quotation from G. K. Chesterton appears on the title page: " 'We only know that the last sad squires ride slowly towards the sea/ And a new people takes the land. . . .' "[7] Thus the demise of the House of Alard parallels the demise of the ruling class in England, and the end comes about through both external and internal causes.

One of the external causes lies in the inability of Sir John Alard to acknowledge that the old order passes, as he looks to Peter to marry an heiress to bring the family out of its difficulties. Despite his "possession of a huge ramshackle estate, heavily mortgaged, crushingly taxed,"[8] Sir John, descendant of the Alards buried in Winchelsea church with "lions at their feet" (3), wields the power implicit in the lions. He was about thirty years old "when he began to reign" (4). A despot, he can brook no opposition, nor can he understand a life apart from the Alard traditions.

Like his father, Peter Alard believes that the family estate must certainly be preserved. He realizes that his brother, Hugh, unfortunately, "had never loved the place as he did—he had never been both transported and abased by his honour of inheritance" (19). The honor, of course, comes through his succession from a long line of Alards. Peter's eyes of "outstanding blue" are "Saxon eyes, the eyes of Alards who had gone to the Crusades, melted down their plate for the White King, refused to take the oath of allegiance to Dutch William; eyes which for long generations had looked out on the marshes of Winchelsea" (8). The abasement comes from his recognition of the necessity of giving up, for a mercenary reason, Stella Mount, the woman he loves and the woman who loves him. He must seek, find, court, and marry an heiress, for only his sacrifice of himself and of his love will save the House of Alard.

Gervase, a young idealist, cannot understand Peter's acceptance of the sacrifice, and it makes him fear for his own future, because "the things over which people agonized were, after all, small shoddy things—earth and halfpence; to see them have such power to crush hopes and deform lives was like seeing a noble tree eaten up by insects. In time he would be eaten up. . . . No, No! He must save himself . . . must find happiness somewhere, But how?" (38). Yet Peter's plight puts Gervase on guard, and his natural bent for mechanics brings him to the point at which he can escape. As well as his escape from living the life of a squire's son, the repair shop work brings him into contact with "all sorts of men, rough and smooth," so that he no longer feels "irrevocably shut up in a class, a cult, a tradition" (40). He has escaped into a larger world.

Although Peter, through his war service, did meet all sorts of men, there was a difference. Peter was an officer, and the military carried on the same class difference with which he had grown up. Gervase works side by side, not above, the men at the garage. In addition, he is fifteen years younger than Peter and a whole generation away in outlook.

Unlike Gervase, Peter feels the weight of untold generations pressing upon him, for "the Family did not merely stand for those at Conster now, but for Alards dead and gone. . . . If Conster had to be sold . . . it would not be only the family now sitting at luncheon that would rise and upbraid him, but all those who slept in Leasan Churchyard and in the south aisle at Winchelsea" (43). He remains the link between the living and the dead Alards. So convinced does he become of his part in this family tree that it takes precedence over his love for Stella, for "if he lost Stella he lost joy, warmth, laughter, love, and the last of youth—if he lost Alard he lost the First and Last Things of his life, the very rock on which it stood" (45).

Peter Alard resembles both Reuben Backfield and Edward Monypenny in his zeal to embrace a cause for which he will be required to give up his own comfort. As they both give up love to attain a more than human goal, so Peter renounces love for a like goal, the creation of himself as an Alard, linked both to the past and to the present.

Feeling the necessity of rationalizing his decision (like Backfield and Monypenny), Peter uses Mary's words—" 'And yet I married for love' "—to cement his decision. He tells himself that love is "as uncertain as everything else—it came and it was gone"(63). He tells himself that he cannot "fail the centuries for what might not live for more than a few years" (64). And he tells Stella, finally, that what he is doing is " 'only half selfish—the other half is unselfish, it's sacrifice' " (67).

But his love for Stella does last, and his sacrifice of this love for the sake of the House of Alard fails to sustain him. His jealousy of Gervase's friendship with Stella undermines the security the Alard family gives him. A further undermining of his security comes in the realization that he does not yet have an heir to the Alard name. He wonders whether it is the war that has shaken his security, but then, he "caught uneasy glimpses of another reason, hidden deeper . . . a vague sense that it would be awful to have sacrificed so much for Alard and Starvecrow, and find his sacrifice in vain—to have given up Stella Mount (who would certainly not have given him a book instead of a baby) only that his brother Gervase might some day degrade Alard, sell Starvecrow and (worst of all) marry Stella" (150).

Peter wants everything—a wealthy wife, Starvecrow as it was before his wife's money changed it, an heir for the Alards—and Stella. He can sustain his life with Vera until she gives birth to a daughter instead of the son he wanted and until he sees Gervase's growing love for Stella. He now realizes that he can never again be a husband to Vera, and thus he will produce no heir for Alard. Despite the fact that he takes to riding a white horse to "emphasize his Squirehood, since to it he had sacrificed himself as freeman and lover" (252), the part of him rooted in loyalty to family disappears. He realizes further that it is Stella to whom he is unfaithful in his marriage to Vera. He has repented and needs to come back to her. He realizes that his sacrifice of himself and Stella is not only not worthwhile, but is also in vain. And he cannot have Stella, for Stella's religion convinces her that adultery is sinful. Although still in love with Peter, she cannot bring herself to commit what she feels is a sin.

In the context of present-day morality, based on fulfillment of the individual rather than on outside sanctions, Stella's refusal of the love that would have saved Peter seems absurd. Yet, given Stella's character, basic to which is a scrupulous regard for religious law (the Ten Commandments), any other course would be outside her character. Even today, many women would decide as Stella did. The rightness or wrongness of the choice depends upon one's values. For Stella (and presumably for Sheila Kaye-Smith), the choice is the proper one, even though it destroys Peter.

Thoroughly disillusioned by the choices he has made, Peter acknowledges to himself that both Jenny and Gervase have chosen rightly in choosing freedom over slavery to family. He is envious of them. But his final despair comes from his realization of what he has made of Starvecrow itself, the land and home for which he had sacrificed what now he has come to see as making life worth living, Stella and her love. "When he thought of that quiet, ancient house, with its bricked floors and wide, sunny spaces, with its humming kitchen fire and salt-riddled beam-work—above all when he thought of it as the home of loving hearts and the peace which follows daring—he felt unendurably the contrast of what he had made of Starvecrow. . . . even if he had renounced the place he loved for the woman he loved, Starvecrow would have still gone on being the same, either as the home of another agent, or . . . the home of some honest farmer" (299–300).

He has, therefore, not only not helped Starvecrow, but he has destroyed it. His actions have had the opposite effect of his intentions. He sees Starvecrow as he has made it. "It was the home of a burnt-out love, of the husks of marriage, of a husband and wife whose hearts were foes and whose souls were strangers, of lost illusions, of dead hopes. . . . and the unchanged, unchanging Stella might have been his instead of this changed Starvecrow" (300). He had felt, governed by illusion, that Starvecrow would never change. Now he knows that his life has been sacrificed to "a dream, a shadow," and "without the substance," it "must go up in smoke." Alard now seems to him a "monster," and he feels himself "worn, tired, disillusioned, shop-soiled, not fit mate for the vivid woman whom some hidden source of romance seemed to keep eternally young." He knows that he had sacrificed Stella three years before when he married Vera, sacrificed her to what he desired then. He can see that "it would be poor atonement to sacrifice her again—to another set of desires" (300–301).

Just as Monypenny must destroy Marlingate, to which he had sacrificed Morgan, so Peter must destroy himself, to whom he had sacrificed Stella. For his desires are the core of his being. He destroys himself because he has betrayed "not only himself, not only Stella, but also Starvecrow" (306). He cannot live with the knowledge of his betrayal, cannot live knowing that he has made all the wrong choices. As he ends his life, he ends the Alard line, the line for the preservation of which he has been brought to his destruction.

The motivation for Peter's primary action in choosing the family over Stella seems clear. Family tradition, family pride, the hint of sacrifice—all combine to help him choose to build what he feels will be solid—Starvecrow, his home; and Conster, the family home of the Alard estate. He learns, through suffering the results of his choice, that what he had believed to be solid was, in fact, rotting from within. Giving up the love of Stella, which would have strengthened him, results in the weakening of the fabric of his being. He knows that "neither the fact that his newborn child was a girl, nor the final defection of Gervase, the heir apparent, could make him hold his breath for Alard. These things had not killed his dreams, as once he had thought, but had merely shown that they were dead" (300). He learns, finally, that there is something stronger than loyalty to tradition and the ego satisfaction that being of the gentry brings and that something is love, with its ability to free the individual from the need for ego satisfaction.

Jenny Alard stands as contrast to Peter. Although her story appears subordinate to Peter's, it shows the result of not allowing class consciousness to rule one's actions. Jenny, faced with the same choice as Peter, refuses to allow the fact that she is an Alard stop her from marrying the man she loves, Ben Godfrey of Fourhouses. She may have married her first love, Jim Parish, had he been wealthy enough to support her, but as he is not, she is doomed either to maidenhood or to seeking a marriage outside of her class. In a society in which money marries money as well as old family (of the upper class) marries old family, the only acceptable deviation is for wealth to make up for the lack of family tree, as in the case of Peter and Vera. Jenny cannot marry within her class, because her family is poor, in spite of its lavish living. In addition, she, like Gervase, is of another generation, a generation which does not find its status in class. She has, also, too much regard for her own happiness to seek to marry to replenish the family fortune.

Jenny is caught in the bind of the two main requirements for marriage among the gentry: she must marry to preserve the family name and traditions (marry within her class), and she must marry another wealthy enough to redeem the family fortune (maintain the proper standard of living). The first requirement might be lifted, as it was in the case of Peter and Vera, if the outsider had sufficient wealth to compensate for his lack of class and also provided he had the wealth from business or industry. To marry a farmer, no matter how prosperous, would be to marry outside of one's class.

Jenny, of course, does marry outside her class and is promptly ostracized by her family and friends. Ben Godfrey has an old family name and a prosperous farm, but he makes a living with his hands. But Jenny is attracted to him, because she has

felt the galling pettiness of the social round, the hollowness of the disguises which her family had adopted, the falseness of the standards which they had set up. . . . She was curious to see the home of the man whose values were not upside down, who had not sacrificed essentials to appearances, who found his pleasure in common things, who, poorer than the poverty of Alard, yet called himself rich. Godfrey had captured her imagination, first no doubt through his virile attraction, but maintaining his hold through the contrast of her brief glimpse of him with the life that was daily disappointing her. (181)

Jenny has not completely broken away from her upbringing when first she meets Ben Godfrey. The residual class consciousness makes it difficult for her to accept him completely. She wonders whether she is truly in love with him and ready to override "the efforts of her class instinct to keep her back" or whether his attraction for her is simply "because she was tired of convention—of county shams—of having to go without things she wanted in order to have things she didn't want." She also wonders whether the latter represents merely "the effort of her mind to justify her heart" (194), for she feels a great attraction to him. She also feels an affinity between her ancestors and his. "She liked his eyes, because they were not the brown bovine eyes of the mixed race who had supplanted the original South

Saxons, but the eyes of the Old People, who had been there before the Norman stirred French syllables into the home-brew of Sussex names. They were the eyes of her own people, though she herself had them not, and they would be the eyes of her children" (197).

The simplicity, the honesty, and the homeliness of Ben's family seal Jenny's choice. "She would always remember that faint sweet scent of freshly ironed linen, that crack of a hidden fire, that slow ticking of a clock—and Ben Godfrey's face before her, so brown, strong and alive, so lovable in its broad comeliness. The last of her reserve dropped from her—he ceased to be a problem, a choice, a stranger; he became just a fond, friendly man, and her heart went out to him as to a lover, forgetting all besides" (198-199).

Added to his physical attraction and the attraction of his home is Ben's maturity in knowing that he is, fundamentally, Jenny's equal. He has no false standards based on class. He knows himself to be a decent person, one worthy of Jenny. Jenny and Ben meet and love as equals.

Jenny does not hide the manifestations of his class from her consciousness. Rather, she accepts them as being part of the person she loves. She laughs at the laborious letter he writes her, with its "freindship"; she shudders at the furnishings of his best parlor; she sees the awkwardness of him in his best clothes. But she also sees that she loves him "all the better for these occasions . . . which seemed to strip him of his splendour and show him to her as something humble, pathetic and dear" (201). She decides to leave the best parlor as it is, even though it is hideously furnished according to the standards of her class. She makes no compromises, but instead, she becomes a farmer's wife, working alongside of Ben, eating her meals with his family and workers, and loving not only her husband, but her life.

Mary points out the difference between Jenny's life and her own, as she tells Jenny, " 'I married a man I loved, a man of my own class, whom my people approved of—and look at me now. You, on the other hand, have taken every imaginable risk—a runaway match, a different class, and the family curse' " (287). Jenny's love for Ben rests on solid ground. Ben's "deference for her was entirely for her as a woman, and he had no particular respect for her as an Alard. . . . He was grateful to her for loving him, and infinitely careful of her love, as a privilege which might be withdrawn, but he saw no condescension in her loving him, no recklessness in her seeking him" (206). And Ben "appealed to [Jenny] as a freeman, because she knew that if she went to him she would be free—free of all the numberless restrictions and distresses that bound her youth" (188). Thus Jenny experiences the freeing power of Ben's love, so that she knows, as his wife, that his life is better than was hers, and she shares it willingly, even ardently.

Mary's life becomes a mockery of the life she had at the beginning of her marriage. Disillusioned over her choice, even though it was the family choice also, she becomes "less Mary Pembroke than a suit of lovely grey velvet and fur which had somehow come alive and taken the simulacrum of a woman to show off its beauty" (274). Not daring to test her freedom, Mary has lost it. Jenny's daring has won her hers. The difference between the lives of the two sisters points up the stifling effect of following family custom and tradition and the liberating effect of daring to do what one knows one must. It becomes a question of courage.

The second underlying theme of *The End of the House of Alard,* that relating to religion, also has to do with courage. Gervase, in his daring to become a garage mechanic, exemplifies some of this courage. His decision, finally, to become an Anglican monk exemplifies this courage carried to its highest degree. His father makes little of Gervase's choice of career, doing nothing more than grumble about it. But in his choice of vocation, not only does Gervase alienate the family, but eventually he causes its end. Yet he dares himself, risks himself as a person, fully knowing the chance he takes in giving his life to God.

The risk of religion, the tremendous need to put himself on the line in the most difficult adventure of all, lies at the root of Gervase's decision. Gervase first repudiates his father's values clearly when Sir John urges him to go to Oxford so that he " 'will pick up some notion of what's done, and get more like other people.' " But Gervase shows a clarity of vision lacking in his father when he replies that he " 'shouldn't get more like other people, only more like other Oxford men' " (22). Rejecting upper class values, Gervase wishes to follow his own inclination, and if this takes him into the life of a garage mechanic, with its long hours and hard work, he feels it is worth all his effort. The family expectations of him have not stifled the strong core of his will

pushing him to achieve his own personality, because he is the
youngest son and not seriously considered as inheritor to the
House of Alard. He can, therefore, ask himself what Peter lacks
which makes him reject Stella for Alard. "How was it possible
that he could stumble at such a choice? What was money,
position, land or inheritance compared to simple solid happiness?" (38). But Gervase has never felt the pull of tradition, the
responsibility to family name and fortune that has been Peter's
lot, for Gervase, through benign family neglect, has been
allowed to find his security in himself instead of in outward
forms.

Mary recognizes that Gervase's hands, full of grime and with
broken fingernails, symbolize "a freedom which was more actual
than any she had made." She knows that he is the only one in the
family who is

really free, though he worked ten hours a day for ten shillings a week.
Doris was not free, for she had accepted the position of idle daughter,
and was bound by all the ropes of a convention which had no substance
in fact. Peter was not free because he had . . . married away from his
real choice, and was now bound to justify his new choice to his heart—
George was not free, he was least free of all, because individual
members of the family had power over him as well as the collective
fetich. . . . Slaves . . . all the Alards were slaves . . . to Alard—to
the convention of the old county family . . . the foundations of which
were rotten right through. (16)

Gervase is truly free. He is calm, careless, and sufficient to make
his own choices.

But although Gervase is free to make his own choices, he is not
free to marry Stella, for Stella is not in love with him. Because of
this, he envies Jenny her happiness, for he sees her happiness as
rooted in what he has wanted for himself, "with double roots in
security and caring." He wonders "if only the kingdom of heaven
was happy in that way, and if he could not find homeliness and
adventure together on earth. He did not want one without the
other, he did not want peace with dullness, nor excitement with
unrest. He had learned that the soul could know adventure with
profoundest quiet—might not the body know it too"? (218).

Gervase, seeking both rest and excitement, finds it in religion.
For him, it becomes the "fulfillment of love." And he finds in
Anglo-Catholicism, what he calls "Catholic Christianity," the

peace and order he has been searching for, a peace and order rooted in the common things of life. He sees that

"Catholic Christianity stands fast because it belongs to an order of things which doesn't change. It's made of the same stuff as our hearts. It's the supernatural satisfaction of all our natural instincts. It doesn't deal with abstractions, but with everyday life. The sacraments are all common things—food, drink, marriage, birth and death. Its highest act of worship is a meal—its most sacred figures are a dying man, and a mother nursing her child. It's traditional in the sense that nature and life are traditional." (233)

One can find, certainly, Sheila Kaye-Smith speaking here, from the mouth of Gervase, her own conviction. And she, through Gervase, also expresses the idea that the earth, like religion, cannot be shaken. The two main themes of the novel meet in Gervase's remark to Jenny that "the land will still be there though the Parsons go. The Parson and the Squire will go, and their places will be taken by the Yeoman and the Priest who were there before them" (234).

Sheila Kaye-Smith's feeling that false values reside both in the squire class and Low Church Anglican religion appears unequivocably here. As she evokes the forcible wrenching out of the Catholic faith in sixteenth century England in *Superstition Corner* and conveys the psychological effects of class differentiation in *The Lardners and the Laurelwoods,* in *The End of the House of Alard* she combines the two themes. What had once been will return, because, in her opinion, there has been a rape of both religion and land.

Gervase's decision to enter Thunder Abbey as a monk stands on his realization that Thunder Abbey is " 'just part of that heart of prayer that keeps the world alive.' " And he feels that his place is " 'in that heart' " (248). Even Stella, who finds her own solace in her faith, envies Gervase, not the peace and definiteness of his choice, but his freedom, because Gervase "made the ultimate surrender and was free. . . . He was beyond her, not because of his vocation, but because of his freedom" (250).

If the story of Gervase is, in part at least, the story of Sheila Kaye-Smith's own conversion to Anglo-Catholicism, the story of George Alard reveals the basis for the conversion. George Alard's conflict centers on his experience of himself as a parson and that of Father Luce as a priest. Although both, technically, belong to the Anglican church and serve under the same bishop, the beliefs under which each operates and the actions through which each administers to those under his care represent great differences. George has always felt that there is something "ungentlemanly" about Catholicism, even though he feels he is broadminded and would have "introduced one or two changes on High Church lines into the services at Leasan if his father and his wife had let him" (104).

George's difficulty with his conscience stems from the conflict between what is expected of him by his wife and family (an external religion, a religion of gentlemen) and his realization that High Church service and symbolism satisfy a deep need of his religious nature. Religion, as he administers it to his parishioners, has always been a matter of work parties, parish teas, and the start of a parochial council, not, as it is to Gervase, "a faith which did not depend on the beauty of externals for its appeal—a faith, moreover, which was not afraid to make itself hard to men, which threw up round itself massive barriers of hardship, and yet within these was warm and sweet and friendly—which was furthermore a complete adventure, a taking of infinite risks, a gateway on unknown dangers" (103).

In this view, one can almost equate Reuben Backfield's daring of his human condition to meet its utmost limits with Gervase's daring of his own human limitations. The instigation appears to be the same. For Reuben Backfield the need is for a triumph over nature; for Gervase the need is for a triumph over himself.

Mary recognizes the difference between George's religion and Father Luce's, the one Stella Mount practices. She tells George that his religion seems " 'chiefly to consist in giving people soup-tickets and coal-tickets, and having rummage sales. Stella Mount's religion at least means an attempt at worship . . . anyhow it makes you want something you haven't got' " (105). Her words lead George to wonder whether it is the devotion he finds in Father Luce's church, with poor farmers kneeling in front of the altar, which makes "the difference between religion and soup" (107).

George, uneasy in his brand of religion, develops "disquieting eccentricities, such as going into the church to pray" (119). As he prays, he finds himself increasingly dissatisfied with his religious life, and he realizes that "the dawn of that dissatisfaction had been in the Leasan Church itself . . . while he was kneeling there alone among all those empty, shining pews." He wonders whether he has "a secret shameful hope" that he will find Luce's church empty if he stops in (122). His feeling that he is competing with Luce indicates his own lack of conviction about his chosen calling.

George's accidental pulling off of the daisy chain hung on the statue of the Virgin Mary perhaps symbolizes his desire to strip the adornments from religion, to make it "empty, shining pews," which would reassure him that his religion is worthwhile. He finds it hard to understand why the "uninspiring" figure of Luce can "make his church a house of prayer," while he cannot make his own church one. He also finds it difficult to understand why "people thought and talked of Luce as a priest" and they thought of him "only as a parson, paid him subscriptions and asked him to tea" (125).

He sees part of the answers to his own questions in learning that Luce is extremely poor, having no outside income to support him, as he himself has. He also sees that the fact that the Blessed Sacrament is kept in the church brings in worshippers, even though Luce assures him that he doesn't keep the Sacrament there "for purposes of theology, but for practical use" (127). Also, the hideous statues make the church homey to people whose best parlors are also "hideous," judged by Anglican good taste. To them, the church is home, as George's church could never be.

But the greatest difference between Luce and himself, perhaps, is the fact that there is "not a sign of tea." George suddenly realizes "as a hitherto undreamed-of possibility that Luce did not take tea" (128). He finds Luce's world a world with a "choking atmosphere . . . in which lived daily communicants, devout children, and clergymen who hadn't always enough to eat." To cap it all, Luce seems "totally unashamed" of his poverty (129).

It is this part of George's Christianity which Gervase finds different from that which he finds in Luce's church. Catholic Christianity, for Gervase, is not just " 'an aid to good behaviour, but something which demanded your whole life, not only in the teeth of what one calls evil, but in the teeth of that very decency and good form and good nature which are the religion of most

Englishmen'" (134-35). Again, it is the equation of good manners, good breeding, upper class, and Low Church; while uneducated, natural, lower class equal High Church. Squire plus Leasan (George's church) oppose yeoman plus Vinehall (Luce's church).

Like Peter, George realizes that his life has been a failure.

As he walked through the thick yellow light of the Hunter's Moon to Leasan, he saw himself as a curiously feeble and ineffective thing. It was not only that he had failed to persuade his brother by convincing arguments, or that he had failed once more to inspire his father with any sort of respect for his office, but he had somehow failed in regard to his own soul, and all his other failures were merely branches of that most bitter root. . . . He had been unable to convince Gervase because he was not convinced himself—he had been unable to inspire his father because he was not inspired himself. All his life he had stood for moderation, toleration, broad-mindedness . . . and here he was, so moderate that no one would believe him, so tolerant that no one would respect him, so broad-minded that the water of life lay as it were stagnant in a wide and shallow pond instead of rushing powerfully between the rocky, narrow banks of a single heart. . . . (137-138)

He knows that Gervase has found "adventure, discipline and joy in faith" (138). He admits that " 'religion is romance' " and that for twelve years he has been trying " 'to turn it into soup' " (139).

The knowledge of his own failure becomes too much for George to bear, just as Peter's knowledge of his failure became too much for him. When his weak heart gives out and he orders that Father Luce be sent for, the Lord comes "suddenly to Leasan Parsonage" in the figure of a "tall stooping figure in a black cloak, under which its arms were folded over something that it carried on its breast" (143). The occasion, therefore, of George's death has accomplished what George could not do during his life—bring the Lord to Leasan parsonage.

The interweaving of the stories of Peter and Stella, George and Gervase, Jenny and Ben, Mary and Doris brings about an alignment of what might be seen as opposing forces. Stella, Jenny, and Gervase represent the power of love to free the individual from the restrictions set by society and family. For Stella and Gervase, love of God is the motivating force. As they surrender themselves completely to God, they free themselves from the hampering restrictions of lesser loves. For Jenny, it is

Ben who acts as the motivating force. Loving him as an equal, she is free to surrender herself to a love which surpasses any self-love she may have gained through the ego satisfaction of class superiority.

The opposing forces of family loyalty and conventional upbringing are represented by Peter, George, Doris, and Mary. Peter's loyalty to family and the ego satisfaction that the knowledge of his position gives him cannot sustain the harsh reality of knowing what he has lost, both in Stella and in Starvecrow. George's adherence to the gentlemanly code cannot sustain him when he sees the reality of a different code: Father Luce's code of poverty, humility, and deep faith. Mary and Doris, both products of a tyrannical father, live lives without love and without hope. Doris cries out at the end of the novel, " 'Oh, Father—oh, Peter. . . . What would you have done if you had known how it was going to end?' " (353).

Of course, that is the crucial question. No one can know. One is reminded of the lesson Albert Speer learned through his relationship with Hitler, that there are no ends, only means.[9] The means, ignored by Sir John Alard, by Reverend George Alard, by Captain Peter Alard, reside in the love evidenced by Stella, by Jenny, and by Gervase. For Sheila Kaye-Smith, the means consist of a love which liberates the creative force of each person to help not only himself but also his neighbor to grow into a mature human being.

Patrick Braybrooke feels that "we are made to feel sorry for the Alards," as "the end of the noble house of Alard is brought about by the Alards. It is in this that Miss Kaye-Smith harps on the tragic, for of all the tragedies that pursue a family, the most tragic is that . . . which makes a family end itself."[10] It is debatable as to whether or not "we are made to feel sorry for the Alards," but certainly the end of the House of Alard is not tragic in the sense of unfortunate, which seems to be Braybrooke's meaning. The tragedy, in the Greek sense, of course, consists in the family's having brought about its own downfall, but the reader is forced into the idea that this is a good thing. The family which exacted the life blood, physically and spiritually, of its members is a family which put prestige, dignity, convention, and class above the individual right of each member to make himself or herself through the development of his or her own gifts.

It must be noted that Sir John's control of the family through his emphasis on tradition destroys what it was designed to promulgate. His ideal might be seen to be a valid one, just as the individual's choice of an ideal for consecration of a life might reside in religion, in social service, or in care of family. It is not the ideal itself which causes the tragedy but rather Sir John's forcing his family into the acceptance of *his* ideal. Sheila Kaye-Smith appears to be saying that each person must follow his or her star. To give up this creative force by accepting another's values leads, for her, to tragedy.

Even though manipulation of plot may be seen here, and Sheila Kaye-Smith has been accused of plot manipulation, all novelists must manipulate to some extent. How they do this makes the difference between the presentation of one view of reality over another. Sheila Kaye-Smith manipulates in order to show, perhaps, the Judaic-Christian value residing in the freedom of the individual to become what he or she has the potentiality of becoming. When one allows another to impose values, tragedy results. The outmoded ideas promulgated by Sir John Alard and his family, which exacted as due the creative impulse of each family member under the dictatorship of Sir John, certainly needed to end. There is no question that Sheila Kaye-Smith thinks so.

III   The View from the Parsonage

Although Sheila Kaye-Smith's view of religion and her adherence to basic Christian tenets do not change from her first acceptance of them until her death, the various aspects of faith, as seen in the believer, occupy her attention. She develops one side of character and then another, as she considers the question of the manifestation of God in the world and each individual's response to it. For example, *The End of the House of Alard* contrasts George Alard with Father Luce and points up George's deficiencies in comparison with Luce. In *The View from the Parsonage,* however, Miss Kaye-Smith presents Parson Carpenter, who remains completely at peace with himself as minister in the Anglican church, even though the story he narrates concerns more the Roman Catholic church than his own. The fact that Miss Kaye-Smith contrasts Roman Catholicism with Anglicanism in *The View from the Parsonage* instead of High Church and Low Church as she does in *The End of the*

House of Alard is merely the result of her conversion to Roman Catholicism. For her, as pointed out above, her conversion was merely a change in "allegiance" and not in basic beliefs.

Harry Chamberlin, parson of the Village of Ebony, narrates the story from the vantage of his nearly fifty years at the parsonage. He says it is the story of Adam Cryall, but in reality, it is also his own. Adam Cryall, who heads one of the two remaining families of gentry (the other is the Lismore family) is an atheist. He had been a clergyman, but he renounced his orders and became an atheist after listening to the arguments of an atheist lecturer he had befriended at the parsonage. He has been forbidden to visit Palster Manor, the Cryall family home, by his father, after his renunciation of orders, but he inherits the manor on the death of his brother in 1887. He comes to live there with his wife Lucy and in 1892 chooses Parson Carpenter to hold the living he had renounced. The two become close friends despite their theological differences.

In Adam Cryall's early days as a clergyman, he had served in London with another clergyman, Edward Boutflower, with whom he had also become friends. Edward Boutflower also renounced his orders, but he did so to enter the Roman Catholic church. The friendship between Adam Cryall and Edward Boutflower endures, however, and when Adam comes into the family fortune, he befriends the Boutflower family by entertaining them frequently at Palster Manor and by financing the education of the Boutflower children.

Adam has two daughters, Blanche and Lindsay, and he brings them up according to his atheistic principles. He is a humanist; good, ethical, and intelligent. Although the story presumably is about Adam Cryall, it is also about his daughter Blanche, whom Parson Carpenter confesses he loves, although he never confesses it to Blanche, who calls him "Uncle Harry."

The narrative passes over many years and resumes when the daughters are grown. Lindsay Cryall, the younger daughter, lacks the beauty and intelligence of her sister and is, therefore, less favored by her father. Her apparent gift of extrasensory perception is ridiculed by Adam, and although she can read minds, she pretends that she makes it all up, not only to keep herself free of her father's ridicule, but also to keep part of herself secret from him, thereby gaining an advantage over him. When her part in a seance at the Lismores apparently brings back the presence of Tom Lismore, presumed dead, she has a sudden conversion and is convinced that God does indeed exist. However, when Tom Lismore returns home alive, she loses this sudden belief in God.

Lindsay later marries Tom Lismore, against the advice of the parson and of her father, for Tom is a n'ere-do-well who has fathered at least two illegitimate children. However, their marriage prospers. Both Lindsay and Tom conform outwardly to the Anglican church, although neither experiences a religious faith. Lindsay apparently loses her extrasensory perception. They live in London and carry on their affairs in contentment.

Blanche Cryall, a highly intelligent woman, is educated by her father and at Cambridge. She falls in love with Anthony Boutflower, but rationally assessing the differences between her atheism and his Roman Catholicism, she gives him up. She marries, instead, George Haffenden, a young farmer who manages one of her father's farms, Church Farm. Her first child is stillborn, which her husband blames on her, as she had gone into the fields to bring some refreshment to the workers instead of sitting and doing nothing as he felt a "lady" who was expecting should. Her second baby dies at the age of one from scarlet fever contracted from the child of the Church Farm looker. Blanche had taken the child and its mother into her home to care for them, not knowing the child was ill, after mother and child had been turned out of their home by the looker. The looker had gone mad after hearing an evangelist lecture.

Blanche, restless with nothing to do, as her husband will not allow her to help with the farm, goes to London a day or two a week to lecture at various schools. After a time, she renews her love affair with Anthony Boutflower, whose wife has rejected him after having a nervous breakdown. Blanche and Anthony run away to Paris. Meg, Anthony's sister, and the parson follow them to Paris. Meg attempts to reason with Anthony, and the parson attempts to reason with Blanche.

The parson's attempt meets with success, and Blanche returns home after Anthony is forced to marry one of Blanche's young students. Blanche converts to Roman Catholicism and joins the Sisterhood of the Poor Clares.

The parson and Adam Cryall continue their friendship until the death of Adam. The parson administers to his parish, enjoying a peaceful and easy life, remaining even after Adam's death and the passing of Palster Manor to outsiders. After World War I, the bishop suggests that the parson retire, but he refuses, and when the story ends, he is seventy-eight and planning to continue the life he has lived for nearly fifty years at the parsonage.

IV   *Innocence and Evil*

The parson, through his narrative, reveals himself as a good, kindly, gossipy man, interested in helping others to come to a reasonable decision about their lives, but not interested in setting either himself or others aflame with worship of God. He is conventional and gentlemanly—an innocent. He acts as he does because he simply has never considered that there is any other way to act. Adam Cryall, on the other hand, is not an innocent, but he is a better person than the parson, considered from a religious point of view, which makes "doing to the least" one of its tenets.

The two friends share the same view, both literally and figuratively, although the figurative view of one is atheistic and that of the other is presumably Christian. When Adam is banished from his home after his renunciation of his ministry, the

view that he remembered with acutest longing was . . . from the field behind the Parsonage. Standing here one could see the house, crouching in the hollow which was its garden and had been its moat, while beyond it the shores of Ebony dropped into the marshes and the sea-born mists. In his dreams he would see it there at his feet.[11]

This, of course, is the parson's view as he looks out of his window.

Both men share a background which has taught them to behave like gentlemen, conventional in expectations and faithful to country mores. But Adam, although he is an atheist, lives a Christian life in daring to act on behalf of those less fortunate than himself, while the parson, outwardly every inch a Christian, takes none of the risks which Christianity requires. Theologically, both argue opposite extremes.

The parson worries that perhaps he should not enjoy his conversations with Adam, that he should be

more distressed by Adam's flippancy, more scandalized by his past, more painfully conscious of the fact that he had once been a clergyman . . . and had renounced his orders, not to follow the well-worn track to Rome but to become a secularist on the Bradlaugh model, a fool who had said not only in his heart but on public platforms, "There is no God." (2)

But the parson needs a friend of his own class, for when he came to Ebony, although he came as a "Sussex man born and bred," he came as a "foreigner," for there had been either a Cryall or a Lismore holding the living for the past four hundred years (4). The parson came to Ebony because he was, up until then, disillusioned by his clerical experience. He muses to himself how different it was from what he expected. He believed he would be

sitting in a Victorian-Gothic study, surrounded by books and emerging only to identify myself in sixteenth-century prose with the sober doctrines of the Church of England, in a building erected by a still older faith. . . . Very different was my actual experience. . . . I found myself bound to a circling wheel of clubs, guilds, choir-practices and house-to-house visiting . . . mainly social. . . . I hated it all, and would have been glad to escape even without the tragedy which speeded my departure. (5)

The "tragedy" consists of his losing the young woman he was engaged to for no other reason than that "'she could not go through with it.'" This implies, perhaps, something about his own character as a minister. For, some years later, "she joined an Anglican sisterhood" (6). Perhaps her brand of religion was superior to his even then.

Ebony is, of course, the perfect place to meet his requirements. And he took the place of a better parson, Adam Cryall. Even though Adam always said that he "took orders for no other reason than to end his days at Palster Rectory," his actions as a beginning clergyman belie his statement. Before coming to Ebony, he, with Edward Boutflower, "two Victorian clergymen in long black frock coats and little round black hats" walked "side by side on the filthy pavements, daring together the courts and the alleys which were shunned by the police," entered "rotten tenements where the stairs broke under their feet and lice and plaster shook down together from the cracked ceilings" (10). They cared for the least of their brethren.

Again when Adam came to Palster Rectory, his "decision to

clean up Jute Street and Sody Street was an act of clerical swashbuckling." Although he was quite successful, "he earned the vengeance of three sections of the community—the vested interests . . . the patrons of those interests . . . and most dangerous of all, the respectable members of his own congregation, who not only resented the undesirable publicity that had been given to their parish, but were jealous of their pastor's preoccupation with the more disreputable members of his flock" (13). Thus Adam represents an ideal clergyman, actively engaged in righting the wrongs society inflicts on the unfortunate. Because he has a keen sense of justice, however, he loses his faith. Because of the injury sustained by William Dale, atheistic lecturer, an injury inflicted by an unruly mob, Adam finds himself listening to, and being convinced by, secularist arguments at his own rectory.

Even though Adam has acted, presumably, out of faith in his zealous efforts both for the poor of London and the poor of his own parish, the faith which has brought his friend Edward Boutflower into the Roman Catholic Church and into poverty, thereby, easily slips from his consciousness. In the opinion of the parson, Adam's beliefs

had never been more than an intellectual disguise for his emotions, and once these were redirected—which in view of all that had happened was not difficult—he could shed as a mere husk the doctrines they had worn. The Christian creeds became part of a complex which included the rebukes of his Diocesan, the bigotry of his congregation, and even the vices of Jute Street and Sody Street. I am convinced that he had no mental or spiritual sense of loss, for he still held all that had made his faith alive—his generosity, his idealism, his loving kindness. (15)

As both Adam Cryall and Edward Boutflower leave their ministries, paradoxically, it is the atheist Adam who dispenses charity to the Christian Edward.

Far more painful to Adam than the loss of his faith was his inability to live at Palster Rectory, or even at Palster Manor. However, his honesty made him acknowledge his loss of belief and renounce his orders, with the accompanying penalty of banishment from Palster, and the years spent until he unexpectedly inherits Palster Manor are lived "precariously" (19).

The parson, although far different as a clergyman than Adam had been, enjoys his life, as he confesses that he manages "to conduct . . . three services on Sunday and preside at the monthly meeting of the Easter vestry without any undue strain on . . . health and intellect" (21). The difference between his and Adam's idea of a parson can be clearly seen. Although presumably not a main character in the novel, the parson reveals himself as having the prejudice and the limitations that Miss Kaye-Smith sees in the Anglican clergy.

Not only does the parson seek a life of ease, enjoying the hospitality of the Cryalls and the Lismores, "lavish of the good things" that he sometimes fears he appreciates "too much," but he also reveals himself as a snob, finding the minister of the nonconformist chapel to be an "ignorant fellow without even the education normally found in those days among Nonconformist pastors," so he keeps "out of the way" (27).

On the other hand, Adam, the atheist, always extends a helping hand and an understanding heart to those less fortunate than himself. He also represents an honest, just person who raises his daughters to the principles he espouses. He considers his very intelligent daughter Blanche "sufficiently well grounded in rationalism to be able to withstand any possible ecclesiastical assaults from Cambridge" (33). It is his training of Blanche and his care of her education which give her the means to act logically and intelligently when faced with the results of her love affair with Anthony.

Even though Blanche has "no Christian preconceptions," she has a "logical mind." While she has "no idea of sacrificing her own and Anthony's happiness to the common good or their personal present to the future of the race," her intelligence must recognize that the parson was right when he told her that Anthony without his religion would not be the Anthony she loves. She finally confesses that after two years of living with Anthony, she has "seen him become somebody quite different from the man [she] fell in love with and hoped to marry" (240).

Thus the parson, along with Adam, has been responsible for Blanche's conversion, although he is, as Adam would have been, horrified when this conversion takes her into the Sisterhood of the Poor Clares. The parson makes Blanche understand that the giving up of one's faith means giving up the foundations of what makes one a certain kind of person, in Anthony's case, the person Blanche loved. Blanche, through her conversion, reaches a plane on which she can offer herself as sacrifice. The best "atonement . . . for robbing Anthony of his Church and his Church of Anthony" is to "offer" herself "in his place" (259).

The logic taught her by her father and the insight given her by the parson lead to Blanche's sacrifice. But the purpose of the sacrifice goes beyond Anthony's wife, his family, or convention. Although she leaves Anthony because she no longer loves him, she converts to Catholicism and gives herself completely to it by joining the Poor Clares because she recognizes the power of religion to make the person, as Catholicism has made Anthony. She experiences this power at her baptism, as she tells the parson, " 'I stood there at the font absolutely pure and sinless after all my sins. It wasn't just the scrubbed cleanness of absolution, but the perfect whiteness of a new creature. For five minutes I was what God had meant me to be' " (258). The power to experience absolute good leads Blanche to give herself completely so that she might work for this good.

On the other hand, Lindsay, who gives promise of a sensitivity to spiritual matters, is not encouraged to pursue her gifts. Actually, Adam treats her as a lesser person because she does not have the beauty and intelligence Blanche has. She becomes, therefore, the atheist her father desires her to be, but without his honesty and his love for fellow creatures. She and Tom Lismore conform outwardly to the tenets of the Church of England, but they do so only outwardly, without conviction, and for the very mundane reason that their son might attend a good school.

The parson's cultivation of a perfect white rose with a gold streak, the papal colors, which he names "Adam Cryall," symbolizes his part in the cultivation of Blanche. It also symbolizes Adam's part in the cultivation of the parson. The parson believes, as Adam did, in "peace and progress and human perfectability—words that nowadays provoke a question if not a smile" (147); he recognizes that it was "largely to Adam" that they "owed this creed" (148). Between them, they have cultivated Blanche, the perfect rose.

Like Reuben Backfield, Adam has been true to his own creed. He lives according to the principles he embraces. So when old age comes to him, it has "fallen on him like a golden cloud, and the whole world shone in the mellow, misty sunshine of his humanism. . . . He believed in mankind, and in return mankind in Ebony believed in Adam" (148). As he nears the end of his life,

he can say, as Reuben Backfield said, that he is content. " 'I've
been very happy . . . I've had a happy life. It's been mostly
summer with me. Yet I'm ready to go, even though I believe
death is the end . . . one or two people—people I love—have
disappointed me. But what is that? They are, like myself, no
more than falling leaves. . . . In these days nobody wants war
or believes it can settle anything' " (229).

The parson points out, later, that "it may have been his
Maker's reward for a good life lived without Him that took Adam
from this world six months before that shot was fired at Sarajevo
and the lights went out" (229). The fact that Adam died
believing in the "perfectibility" of the human race, may be, as
the parson suggests, his reward for his good life. But the fallacy
of his creed, the fallacy which Adam did not live to realize,
becomes clear. Humanity, as a whole, did not reach the state that
Adam had hoped and expected for it. But one individual,
Blanche, achieved the "perfectibility" that humanity as a whole
did not. And that individual reached it, not through atheism, but
through religion. The perfectibility of the individual, as
exemplified by Adam's daughter Blanche and symbolized in the
Adam Cryall rose, exists in her conversion and entrance into the
sisterhood.

The parson has grown in stature, also, through the events
which he has helped to happen. He stands midway between
Adam and Blanche in his religious outlook. Like Adam, he cannot
accept the reality which is, for Sheila Kaye-Smith, the foundation of the Roman Church. But like Blanche, he can feel the pull
of the more ancient religion. In France, he experienced this pull.
He confesses that in "this far country I no longer felt the
shepherd I was at home, but one of the sheep. Yet I cannot call it
a specifically religious experience, or perhaps I might say that for
me then, by some unlikely grace, two worlds that should be one
but have been long parted merged together and for a brief hour
became my paradise" (204). Through this insight, the parson
points up the difference between the Roman church as he
believes it to be and the Anglican church as he has experienced
it; between the High Church and the Low Church. In his church
(Anglican and Low) he is a shepherd; in the other church
(Roman or High Anglican), he would be a sheep.

So, he remains an Anglican parson, telling Blanche, " 'I am a
priest of the Church of England, and I hope to die as I have lived,

her loyal, devoted son; but I am well aware of the difficulties and drawbacks of Anglicanism, and I don't know that I could recommend it to anyone like yourself, coming in from outside, without any previous religious experience. . . . Rome is the Church I should have chosen for you if . . . you could swallow what she teaches' " (257). Of course the parson can't "swallow what she teaches." But Blanche gives him a final lesson when she visits him before leaving for the convent. She says, " 'I'm glad you've taken to cats at last, Uncle Harry . . . there's something so attractive about their wickedness. A priest friend of mine says he keeps one entirely for the theological piquancy of a creature who can be a murderer, and lecher, and a thief, and yet at the same time entirely pleasing to God' " (271). The parson responds by giving her the kiss he feels he should have given her thirty years before, revealing the love for her that he has always carried in his heart.

The parson becomes like Adam Cryall, as he extends his charity to the order she has entered, as Adam had extended his charity to the Boutflowers. Both give to the person or persons they love, even though they reject the creed the loved ones live under. He remains an innocent, never fully experiencing evil, as Blanche has experienced it, through the placing of self before righteousness. The parson sums up Sheila Kaye-Smith's estimate of English parsons—innocent, good, kind, and safe in their view from the parsonage.

W. Gore Allen believes that Sheila Kaye-Smith in this novel "reached the pith of ethical contention between Canterbury and Rome. Canterbury may encourage good people to be better; it does not encourage average people to be good."[12] He further believes that after her conversion to Roman Catholicism, she became a "partner; selecting and rejecting; measuring what was true for her against what was historically proven. . . . To accept the Church's claim is to assert that a crime of spiritual violence was committed against the English people. Seen from this ground, their lack of faith is no longer the result of muddle-headedness or malice; they are distinguished as actors in the oldest and the youngest tragedy on earth—heirs who were robbed and cheated of the birthright."[13] In *The View from the Parsonage*, the good parson is encouraged to be better, but the average person, Blanche, is encouraged to be good. The risk, the daring, the sacrifice of religion is reserved for Roman Catholicism (or High Church Anglicanism), while the safe, the plodding, the expected is reserved for Low Church Anglicanism.

The art of Miss Kaye-Smith has both progressed and deteriorated between *The End of the House of Alard* (1923) and *The View from the Parsonage* (1954). There is progression in the weaving of lives as seen through the eyes of the parson, but there is deterioration in the choice of first person narrator. The fact that the parson tells the story leads to his not only giving his own version of events, but also to his commenting on them. This slows the action and results in a novel that lacks the dramatic intensity of *The End of the House of Alard*, to cite a novel which has some of the same underlying themes.

Although the themes of the two novels are similar, the outcome of the conflicts differs. For example, Jenny marries Ben Godfrey in *Alard*, while Blanche marries George Haffenden in *Parsonage*. But Jenny transcends the boundary of class by becoming a farmer's wife, while Blanche, prevented from becoming a farmer's wife by a husband who basks in her stature, cannot sustain the useless life. Further, the love between Jenny and Ben is a love between equals, each secure in themselves, while the love between Blanche and George Haffenden has its basis solely in sexual attraction plus a means to status on George's part. George Haffenden does not see himself as Blanche's equal but rather as beneath her. He therefore forbids her to help with the farm, forcing her into a life of idleness in which she can act neither as a member of the gentry nor as a member of the farming class. As he puts her on a pedestal, he demeans her ability to become a true helpmate.

In addition, the two parsons operate from different religious vantage points. George Alard, parson of Leasan, finds his conflicts in the realm of religion. The emphasis rests on the difference between the Low Church brand of George and the High Church brand of Father Luce. He realizes, finally, that he is not, in reality, the priest he knows he should be. Parson Carpenter, however, experiences no conflict regarding his calling. Aside from the slight twinge he reveals when he describes his feeling in France and when he accepts, reluctantly, the news of Blanche's conversion to Roman Catholicism, he appears to be perfectly satisfied with his calling and with his life. The cat may, of course, help him to reflect on Blanche's comment about it, but the reader leaves the parson with the feeling that he is content, but basically ineffectual, as parson.

Although Reuben Backfield may be seen as an atheist (or at least a person who has rejected all Christian tenets) who is destructive to others, Adam Cryall may be seen as less the atheist he avows to be than the natural man practicing Christian tenets without the underlying beliefs which give them their authority. For the most part, he exhibits constructive behavior, attempting to make his daughters strong, honest, and self-sufficient. He practices what he preaches and, in his good life, helps his neighbor by respecting both him and life itself.

In addition, although Gervase in *Alard* has reached conversion to High Anglicanism and to monkhood through the observation of, and experience with, Stella, a very good person, Blanche in *Parsonage* has come to conversion to Roman Catholicism and to sisterhood primarily through the observation of, and experience with, Anthony, a very weak person. Gervase enters the monastery not to atone, but to experience high adventure. Blanche enters the sisterhood to atone.

Those critics, therefore, who feel that Sheila Kaye-Smith tells the same story again and again, fail to observe the angle from which she views characters and events and fail to note that this angle constantly changes. Although *The End of the House of Alard* is a faster moving story and a more dramatic one, *The View from the Parsonage* is a more subtle story and a more philosophical one. It also exhibits a greater maturity of vision than *Alard*. Perhaps it also requires a greater maturity of vision in its reader.

CHAPTER 6

The Matter of Class

AS James W. Tuttleton points out, the "function of the novelist has always been, and is now, to observe and to order the social facts about us and to dramatize them in a new imaginative interpretation of human experience."[1] In this way, all traditional novels may be seen to be novels of manners. Tuttleton goes on to say that "the novel of manners is primarily concerned with social conventions as they impinge upon character."[2] Social conventions, of course, have primarily to do with class.

The class structure of British society appears in all of the novels of Sheila Kaye-Smith, as class structure, indeed, appears in most traditional novels. In Miss Kaye-Smith's novels, the classes described are ordinarily those of the laboring farmers and the "gentry," the landowners and squires. In *Sussex Gorse* and *Susan Spray*, the protagonists act within their class, while in *Tamarisk Town, Joanna Godden,* and *The End of the House of Alard*, the conflict revolves primarily around the fact that the main actors are of different classes. In *The View from the Parsonage*, the religious conflict overshadows the class struggle, but the underlying power of class structure appears clearly, as the parson recognizes only the Cryalls and the Lismores as his equals. Also, although a great religious gulf divides the Boutflowers and the Cryalls, the families, being of the same class, hold to their friendship.

It is recognized that changes have come about in the twentieth century, but although the "upstairs-downstairs"[3] class situation has almost completely disappeared and the "media seem generally indifferent to the real pluralism of our national life,"[4] class differences, perhaps more than any other, still divide society. Even though people "passively prefer to be indoctrinated in the belief that there are not any real social differences"[5] they "still acknowledge the persistence of the class structure, still detect the signs of class and status, still experience the influence of institutional structures on . . . manners."[6]

Class differences, then, have not disappeared. The sociologist might study them, chart them, and attempt to explain them, but a novelist such as Sheila Kaye-Smith can present them in such a way that the reader can experience them through understanding the human need which either accepts these class differences or rebels against them.[7] Both *The Lardners and the Laurelwoods* (1947) and *Mrs. Gailey* (1951) find their plot and the motivation of their characters in class differences. Miss Kaye-Smith probes the psychological basis for these differences, not condemning either the lower or the upper class for their actions. Rather, as pointed out by E. D. Pendry, "she sees class-differences as the material of tragedy, on both sides."[8] Although *The Lardners and the Laurelwoods* does not end in the tragedy of suicide, as do *Tamarisk Town* and *The End of the House of Alard*, unfortunate events caused primarily by class differences do prevent the characters from reaching maturity as constructive social beings. And Lesley Bullen's suicide in *Mrs. Gailey* might well be laid at the door which separates the classes. The story of the Lardners and the Laurelwoods, who become closely connected in friendship while still retaining social separateness, gives an emotional understanding of what being a member of each class means, while the story of Mrs. Gailey leads to insight into the destruction of an individual who attempts to rise from the class into which she was born.

I   The Lardners and the Laurelwoods

The Lardners and the Laurelwoods is divided into eight parts: a Prelude, three Interludes, and between these, the story told from the point of view of each of four of the characters—Bess and Dick Lardner and Diana and Frances Laurelwood. The Prelude and the Interludes take place in the present (1936); the rest of the novel takes place twenty-four years before (1912).

In the Prelude, Martin Laurelwood arrives at Idolsfold, summoned there because his mother, vacationing at Idolsfold with his two children, has had a heart attack. His sisters, Meg and Diana, are already there. He recalls the summers he had spent there with his family, every summer until the one of 1912.

The story shifts back to 1912. Bess Lardner and Meg

Laurelwood are about nine years old and are close friends. Meg admires Bess and the penny toys she keeps in a little closet. However, this summer, Meg arrives with a very expensive French doll. Bess covets the doll, while Meg covets a toy watch of Bess' costing twopence. Meg wants the watch so much that she exchanges her doll for it. The children hide the doll, knowing that both families would be horrified at the exchange. Bess plays with the doll surreptitiously, not allowing Meg to touch it.

When the hiding place of the doll is discovered, both Bess and Meg are punished, although Bess more severely than Meg. Bess must give back the doll, and Meg must give back the watch. Neither child wishes to do this. Forced to return the watch, Meg throws it at Bess and breaks it. Bess takes the returned doll from Meg's drawer, meaning to destroy it. Discovered in her act, she is forced to return the doll once more to Meg.

In an Interlude, the story shifts to the present and to Diana Laurelwood, now middle-aged. She recalls her love affair with Dick Lardner. Dick, now an alcoholic, has never married and lives with his sister Bess, now married to George Hovenden, at Idolsfold. Diana wishes to verify her own desirability by visiting Sir Humphrey Mallenden, who had been attracted to her twenty-four years before. The discovery that he doesn't recall his former infatuation, nor apparently even know who she is, frightens her and makes her wonder whether what had happened to her years ago was real.

The flashback is to Diana's experience during her last summer spent at Idolsfold (1912). Disappointed with not receiving an expected proposal from a young man, Diana flirts with Dick Lardner, sensitive, artistic, and attracted to her. After Dick falls in love with her, she gives him up, realizing the difference in class between them.

The Interlude presents the Lardner and the Laurelwood children engaging in the same friendship as their parents had before them. Martin Laurelwood fears this intimacy and plans to prevent their coming back to Idolsfold in the future. Diana, seeing Dick again, believes he may still be in love with her, which bolsters her self-esteem. The mystery of why the Laurelwoods suddenly stopped coming to Idolsfold after the summer of 1912 runs as an undercurrent.

Dick Lardner's story concerns the events inherent in Diana's experience, but from his point of view. In his agony over Diana's rejection of him, he seeks solace in drink, a habit which continues into the present.

The Interlude tells of the friendship between Mr. Laurelwood (who had died eight years before the present) and the curate's wife, Mrs. Brown, a flamboyant woman much gossiped about. Mr. Laurelwood, an amateur artist, appreciated the criticism of his work offered by Mrs. Brown. Mr. Laurelwood had left many of his paintings at the Lardners', and Dick has hung them in his room. When the paintings are mentioned, Mrs. Laurelwood becomes agitated and refuses to answer any questions about the summer of 1912.

Diana feels that Dick ought to go away for psychological treatment to cure his alcoholism, as she blames herself for his condition. Bess becomes enraged at the suggestion. Dick can now regard Diana with distaste, if not outright dislike, and indifference.

The final part of the novel concerns the point of view of Mrs. Laurelwood and goes back to the summer of 1912. Noting her husband's interest in Mrs. Brown, she builds up in her mind the notion that he is in love with Mrs. Brown. At the suggestion of Mrs. Lardner, who shares her belief in the danger of the relationship, she goes to see Mrs. Brown to ask her not to come to visit her husband, who had planned to show her his paintings. Mrs. Brown agrees readily, and with amusement, not to come, making Mrs. Laurelwood feel foolish.

When the day comes for the planned tea, Mrs. Laurelwood cannot bear to see the disappointment of her husband when Mrs. Brown doesn't arrive. She leaves the house and rides a bicycle to the home of Mrs. Brown for the purpose of begging her to come, but Mrs. Brown is out. Although she confesses why she had gone to Mrs. Brown's, she does not tell her husband the real reason why she wished to persuade Mrs. Brown to come, merely saying that she could not stand his disappointment. Her husband tells her she is wonderful, never suspecting that she is the real reason for his disappointment.

For the first time Mrs. Laurelwood is glad to leave Idolsfold, and the story ends with the departure of the family, saying they will be back next summer, but never returning until twenty-four years later.

II *Keeping One's Place*

Martin Laurelwood's reflection, as he rides the little train in to the station, that it is "queer how places seemed to hold and keep the emotions which charged them"[9] might be seen to represent the underlying theme of *The Lardners and the Laurelwoods.* The present (1936) can only be understood in terms of the past (1912). But the characters and their relationships have changed, so that Bess Hovenden, meeting Martin after twenty-four years, can think that "it seemed as if he had been nicer as a boy than he was as a man, more kind, more natural" (5). And Meg can remark, " 'Poor Bess! I've tried in vain to find in her a single vestige of the little girl who used to be my heroine' " (7).

The story of that last summer of the Laurelwood's visit, then, supplies the motivation for the later lives of Dick Lardner and Diana Laurelwood, as it also solves the mystery of why, after so many delightful summers at Idolsfold, the Laurelwoods never returned in twenty-four years. Also, viewing the emotions of nine year olds such as Bess and Meg brings to light motivations for actions also valid in adults, [10] such as Bess' desire for power over Meg, and Diana's desire for power over Dick.

But desire for power remains an effect of the separation of the classes rather than a cause of it. There is an attraction of one class for another, and this attraction, on the part of the Lardners, resides in their need to be part of, although only a serving part of, those they consider to be above them, to partake vicariously of a more glamorous life than their own. Mrs. Lardner (in 1912) calls them "the Family" and feels honored to serve them, even though it means upsetting the routine of her own family life and taking on more work for herself. Bess Hovenden (in 1936) still willingly carries on some of the service formerly given to the Laurel-woods, but she loses completely the small residue of respect she has for them on hearing her children called "louts" by Martin. Although she had once been forced to call the Laurelwood child "Miss Meg," she knows that neither she, nor her husband, nor her children will ever emphasize the gap between them by this manner of address. The changing times have provided a different outlook, but only in the lower class, represented by the Lardners. The Laurelwoods, symbol of the upper class, still adhere to class distinctions, finding them, as do the privileged of all times, much to their advantage.

The relationship between Bess Lardner and Meg Laurelwood points up some of the attraction of one class for the other. Meg, secure in her position of being upper class, of being the one served, can freely love and admire Bess and Bess' toys. The Lardners' lifestyle, so different from her own, captivates her with its freedom from the rules of a codified society. Meg envies "the Lardner tea table—she had sardines only occasionally at breakfast and had never eaten a raw onion in her life" (30). And the tea table is not all that Meg envies, for Bess has made it her business to insure her own ego satisfaction by looking down on the Laurelwoods and working to make Meg admire her. "Bess despised her mother and sister's attitude toward the visitors. They talked as if they got something for themselves out of their possessions, triumphs and pleasures. . . . She was the only person in the family who did not envy the Laurelwoods. She knew better—she had made them (in the person of Meg) envy her" (31).

Meg's beautiful French doll, because it represents beauty as well as wealth, poses a distinct threat to Bess' superiority over Meg. Fortunately for Bess, however, Bess' inexpensive toys enchant Meg, and the twopenny watch so entrances her that she can trade the doll for the watch. Bess can, therefore, force Meg into the same inferior position her own mother and sister are forced into. Her ego forces her into arranging the trade of the watch for the doll, because the superiority of Meg (because of her ownership of the doll) has destroyed the ego satisfaction she ordinarily finds in Meg's visit.

There had always been certain drawbacks—having to listen to all the silly talk about them, having to change her dress and brush her hair more often, having to do more housework, having to keep quiet. . . . But Meg had always been sufficient of herself to make a summer treat. In other years, Bess had enjoyed going out with Meg, playing with Meg, showing off to Meg. This year . . . she had done scarcely any of these things. She knew it was her own fault. . . . Those toys which in other years had been her proudest display had been robbed of their glory by that miserable doll. It was because of that miserable doll that she could not enjoy Meg's society. (41–42)

Unlike her mother and sisters, Bess can find no ego satisfaction in the attributes or in the possessions of Meg. Her satisfaction comes from upstaging Meg. By making little of Meg and her possessions, she can compensate for the fact that Meg must be respected by being called "Miss Meg" and must be given first place, even with Bess' own mother and sister.

But Bess is a realist. She will not acknowledge to herself that she is inferior to Meg, even though the actions of her family continually point to the superiority of the Laurelwoods. These actions require that she in turn salve her ego by making herself superior to her friend. The twopenny watch gives her this superiority, for "nothing would persuade her to part with the toy which had so wonderfully restored her to her lost self-esteem" (44). The watch itself means little to Bess. But if she gives it to Meg, she will lose "the power and the glory, returning to her old longing for that beautiful doll, which she could forget only because its owner preferred this thing of hers" (45-46).

Bess has her own devious morality. She remembers the commandment not to covet. If she gives the watch to Meg, she will "covet Veronique." It wouldn't be, really, "kind and unselfish of her" to give up the watch, for she "couldn't do both—give up the watch and not covet the doll. It was too much for anyone, even God, to expect" (45-46).

Meg, being designated superior by both society and the Lardners (with the exception of Bess), has no need to compensate for a feeling of inferiority. She can covet the watch and can, without compunction, swap the doll for it. Bess' ego leaps until she experiences the ecstasy of playing with the doll, her own now. She denies Meg any contact with the doll except to fetch and carry bath water, thus acting as a servant to the doll and to her and "with luck there would still be many more of those happy hours when she was the lady with a dear little girl and Meg was the servant who was not allowed to touch her, only to fetch and carry, to dust and sweep; and there would be many more of those hours more precious still when she sat alone, hugging her darling baby in her arms, not proud, not showing off, just cuddling and loving" (52-53). Bess can forget her need to show her superiority over Meg in her love for the doll, because her love has released her need for ego satisfaction. In loving, she has lost her sense of inferiority.

But Bess' progress upward to security in herself is short-lived, as the adult world forces its own standards on the children. Even though Granny's friend, Joe Morris, indicates that Bess " 'don't

know her place . . . and she'll just have to larn it,' " Bess knows
that her place must be one in which envy of Meg does not
strangle her. She must, therefore, destroy that which makes her
envious of Meg, Veronique, the doll, which she has renamed
"Mathilda."

A broken Mathilda would mean the end of all her troubles, for there
would be nothing any more to make her envy Meg, nothing any more to
give her this pain of loss and longing; and into the bargain she would
have a very handsome revenge . . . she must get rid of Mathilda—put
her right out of the world—or she would never be happy again and
enjoy playing about the place or doing her brushwork at school or
buying toys at Mrs. Austin's. She would never be able to enjoy any of
these things while Mathilda was in the house; so Mathilda must go—she
must be destroyed. (64)

Further, Bess transfers her own self-loathing to her family and
the Laurelwoods. "She hated everyone—all her family and all
the Laurelwoods. Because it was their fault she was having to do
this—having to drown Mathilda. If only they hadn't been so
unkind and so unfair" (65).

It is thus that Sheila Kaye-Smith shows the envy, caused by the
need to feel superior because of low ego, which leads to
violence. Although the one who experiences the blow to her ego
is only nine years old, the feeling might be the same at nine or
ninety. Through the story of Bess' need, the emotional need
which results in violence can be understood. Bess would rather
destroy Mathilda, the doll she truly loves, than experience the
real pain of envy. She tells Dick, " 'I don't want Mathilda to be in
the world any more—it hurts me too much' " (66). Low ego, then,
causes Bess to destroy the object which had compensated for her
feeling of inferiority to Meg, as she knows that the envy over the
doll will be too much for her to bear. Meg is seen here as the
superior child, for, content with her picture of herself (a picture
reinforced by the subservient attitude of the Lardners), she has
no need to compensate either for her place in society or for her
place in her family's esteem. Sheila Kaye-Smith gives, in the
story of the children Bess and Meg, an emotional understanding
of the destructive effect of a low ego, in this case an effect of the
class system which causes it.

III   *The Loss of Beauty*

Like his little sister Bess, Dick Lardner must also give up a
cherished gift, a gift which has enhanced the world for him, just
as the doll was done for Bess. This gift is the love of Diana
Laurelwood. Even though Diana, musing on her love affair with
Dick from the vantage point of twenty-four years later, can
admit to herself that "there had been something in those kisses
which no other man's since . . ." (72), she has to give him up
because she is "'not the sort of girl who marries a farmer'"
(132).

But like Bess, Diana must have power over Dick, not being
satisfied with the admiration she finds in him. Asking him to
clean her bicycle, she makes the request "a test of her power,
and never had her bicycle looked so trim and shining" (105). Yet
his "dumb and blushing gazes were not a currency her exchange
could honor," and she "grew a little impatient when he offered
no more" (105). She needs more. She knows that it "would be a
most refreshing tonic for her self-respect if she could break
down his shyness and make him openly her slave" (106).

Diana's self-respect needs a tonic because, not only is she at
the vulnerable age of eighteen, but she has been disappointed
that an offer of marriage has not come from one of her beaux.
Also, she leads an unexciting life at Idolsfold, and the prospect of
charming Dick Lardner gives zest to her life. Dick is, also,
different from the usual run of farm boys, different also from his
brothers Joe and Clarence. His sensitivity raises him above the
others, in her eyes, and makes him a fit subject for her
blandishments. Not only is Dick the best looking of the Lardners,
but he

had about him an air of refinement which contrasted with the
loutishness of his older and younger brothers. She had heard him
derided in past years for being "girlish" and "namby-pamby." He
brought into farm life a sensitiveness which outraged other workers.
She remembered a very angry scene when as a boy of twelve he had
cried at the marketing of some favorite ducks. . . . He would pick wild
flowers while supposed to be at work, he loved to read. . . . Mr.
Laurelwood said that Dick himself would have liked to paint and he
would have been glad to teach him, but his father had been shocked at
the idea. He didn't want him "made any worse." (105)

Thus the very attributes which make Dick attractive to Diana become the cause of his downfall, if spending an uproductive life as an alcoholic can be called a "downfall." Had Dick not been the attractive person he was, unlike the usual young men of his class, Diana would not have been drawn to him, would not have built up his hopes for marriage with her. Of course, Mr. Lardner's insistence that such things as painting are fine only for the gentry such as Mr. Laurelwood indicates his need to categorize on the basis of class.

Noticing the difference between Dick and the other young men who work at the farm at Idolsfold, Diana reflects that Dick "must be a throw-back to some earlier generations of Lardners, because most of these old country families had good blood in them" (108). The arrogant, patronizing insistence on her own superiority over Dick can nowhere be more clearly observed.

The harvest day picnic, "a day in which the families were supposed to meet on the same ground" and without "social barriers or class distinction" (109), provides the opportunity for Diana's scheme for gaining Dick's love. Of course, the harvest day picnic really cements the differences between the classes instead of removing them. The bestowing of favors by the gentry points up the undisputed fact that they have favors to bestow.

Dick does not know the rules of the game of dalliance in love as played by Diana in polite society. But he knows that he has "no right to be talking" to her as he is, for he knows that his mother and father "would never forgive" him "if they found out about it." So Diana, acknowledging Dick's lower status, knows that "she must be more encouraging than she would have thought it nice to be to a man of her own class" (110).

Thus Diana, caught up in her own need for admiration, sees "her own loveliness gazing back at her out of his eyes (111) as she drifts into lovers' meetings. She revels in "ecstasies" while at the same time she feels that Dick's behavior is "presumptuous" (115). But she grows "hungry" for his lovemaking, finding him "too timid" and "too decorous." Then she experiences "seesaw days, when she repented in the morning of what in the evening had seemed almost holy in its beauty and bliss" (118). Finally, she cannot be "happy without his kisses, she lived by them more intently than she lived for his admiration, his faltering praises of her loveliness" (119).

Diana, then, grows in sensual need for Dick, while Dick grows in love for Diana. She realizes, as he does not, that although they behave like an engaged couple, their lovemaking cannot lead to marriage. She knows that she can never be a part of the Lardner life, as she would have to be were she to marry Dick. "The regard of Lardner for Laurelwood and Laurelwood for Lardner was based on the maintenance of two separate social strata, and their fusion might well swallow up her world" (119). Humphrey Mallender, at the Mallender's party, restores her to her own world once more. She knows that he has "wiped out Dick Lardner as the sun wipes out the moon," and she is now "at ease in daylight, safe back in the comforts and elegancies of her own world, and the terrors of the night seemed both monstrous and degrading in her memory" (130).

Unlike Jenny Alard, who dares to find her reality in becoming the wife of a yeoman farmer, Diana seeks the safe world of elegance and convention, little realizing that she will become, not an authentic person, but merely an automaton following conventional dictates. But she does realize that while she has been drifting along with Dick, accepting his caresses because they brought her sensual satisfaction, he has "not been drifting at all, but steering, planning." Of the two who make love in the moonlight, "only one had been a sensual dreamer, and that one had not been poor, simple, rustic Dick Lardner, but elegant, well-bred Diana Laurelwood" (132). She knows that she must "push him out of her mind and slam the door." If she does that, she will be able to believe that she "had not quite broken his heart—that in time he would recover and see the folly of his hopes as well as the wisdom of her actions" (135).

But she cannot prevent the breaking of Dick's heart, for "no one but Diana had the power to destroy all the beauty and meaning of life and leave him nothing but dead nights and days" (176). Also he knows "how much he had lost besides Diana. Beautiful things like the moon were dead or changed to cruelty" (182). Diana has "robbed" him of "his dreams" (193).

Just as Bess finds people, as well as herself, hateful when she loses the beautiful doll which had helped start to turn her into a loving creature, so Dick finds the world unbearable when he loses the love which had helped him start to find himself through the need to work hard to provide a home fit for Diana. Dick finds that Bess' disgrace is "in one way blacker than his, for unlike him she had sinned against the Laurelwoods" (196). Thus the Laurelwoods are equated with God.

Dick, therefore, attempts to find solace in drink, and all of his glorious gifts of sensitivity, of art, of perception, and of love drain away into a wasted life. But Diana's potentialities also waste away. When Dick sees her again, after twenty-four years, he finds her voice "unnatural," and when he looks at her, he thinks of "those manikins in clothes-shop windows." Although she wears "good clothes" and wears them "well," she does not "look alive" (145). She is like a "dressed-up doll, and old . . . for all her young looks she seemed old, older than Bess, older than Emmy. An old doll. . . . He could hardly believe that he had ever loved her and broken his heart over her" (147).

Again Diana is equated with Veronique (Mathilda), the doll over which Bess broke her heart. But Bess' pain is apparently short-lived, for she finds apparent contentment as the wife of George Hovenden. But Bess is a realist, not a dreamer like Dick. She fights for her right to live in freedom, and if the choice of George Hovenden for a husband keeps her in her class, undoubtedly that is because that is what she sees as desirable.

But Dick is another matter. Even though both Dick and Diana pay in later life for their youthful attraction for each other, Dick pays to a greater extent. Dick wants, not the prestige of the Laurelwoods, but the advantages which come naturally to people of the Laurelwood class. Dick finds the Laurelwoods attractive because they stand "at the opposite poles of his life from the Hovendens" (164) and the Hovendens had come, in his mind

to stand for all that separated him from the things he wanted to enjoy — for all that was coarse and ugly and frightening in his life. The world seemed to be full of them, Hovendens of all ages, following him down the years. At school they had tried to prevent him listening to the teacher — they called him sappy babby — and they hated him to pick flowers. . . . He hated the Hovendens. (163)

On the other hand, the Laurelwoods represent

a world of interest and beauty which existed only in the summer. In summer they came to Idolsfold with their nice, well-fitting clothes, their clean hands and faces, their shining hair, their gentle voices and courteous manners. Nothing about any of them, at any age, was rough or

terrifying. . . . Mrs. Laurelwood always spoke to him nicely, and Mr.
Laurelwood seemed to open a world of beauty with his paintings. The
little girls were pretty and dainty, even when they screamed and ran
about, and Martin was another doorkeeper with a golden key. (164)

Thus Dick recognizes the superiority of a world from which he
is shut out. The Hovendens represent the world he has been born
into—the crude, rough world of the working farmer. He yearns
for the culture, the education, the gentleness of the world of the
Laurelwoods. The Laurelwoods can afford to be gracious, to be
clean, to be quiet—to be all the things Dick admires—because
they do not have to wrest a living from the soil. The Lardners
cannot afford the luxury of sensitivity, for if they were like Dick,
who "anguished for calves separated from their mothers" (105)
and who could not bear to send pet ducks to market, they could
not survive, nor could the Laurelwoods. Dick aspires to a world
into which he will comfortably fit, but the world, in the person of
Diana (and her parents), will not have him. Rejected and
unhappy over the loss of his dreams, he destroys the person he
could have been, and he lives a parasitical life as an alcoholic.

Diana has accepted her world. But her world is not all that
Dick believes it to be, indeed might have been for him. In that
world, conventional behavior brings its own heartaches. The
reader is not told the story of Diana which makes her less a
person than a mannikin, but some of the difficulties of living in
the world of the Laurelwoods can be understood by looking at
Mrs. Laurelwood.

IV   *The Loss of Love*

When Sheila Kaye-Smith was interviewed about the problem
of reconstruction of European nations after World War II and
about the problem of establishing social improvements in
England, she expressed the hope that England's defeat of
totalitarian nations would not result in a form of totalitarianism
for England. She strongly believed that personal liberties must
transcend any governmental or political considerations.[11] This
idea is preeminent in her stories, particularly those in which the
class structure (and what is this but governmental or political
considerations filtered down into social mores) prohibits the
individual free choice. Dick Lardner has no personal liberty, for

his place in the world has been settled by his birth into a lower class. Although his sister Bess recognizes the values in her lower class life and remains satisfied with them, Dick sees a greater value in a class to which he cannot aspire. His fetters are forged by a class structure which forces him to subvert his sensitive and artistic nature, because people of his class ordinarily lack this nature.

Another kind of freedom is lost by Mrs. Laurelwood and, indeed, by Mr. Laurelwood also through class structure. Frances Laurelwood provides the means through which an understanding of the upper class and its problems might be achieved. Frances Laurelwood, as a young bride who spent her honeymoon at Idolsfold, remembers the unhappy first night of her marriage. Hampered by Victorian convention which refused to allow her knowledge of the sexual side of marriage, she experiences deep "disillusion" and "desolation" which "beat their wings over her." She does not know exactly what she had expected, except that "it had been something worthy of the night, worthy of the stars." Only the thought of Mrs. Lardner brings her comfort, for Mrs. Lardner "had been through all this and seemed content." She muses that probably Mrs. Lardner's "expectations had not been so high—the lower orders . . . had not much imagination—but no doubt she too had had her disappointments, her recoils, her regrets. Yet she was obviously a happy woman, happy in her husband and home and children" (221).

Through Frances Laurelwood's wedding night can be seen the attraction Mrs. Lardner has for her. Deep within herself, Mrs. Lardner stands as security. The thought of her brings her comfort. If Mrs. Lardner can withstand the disappointments of marriage, so can she. Mrs. Lardner will help her achieve the serenity she needs to carry on an outward show of love and devotion to a husband she may not even love.

Mrs. Lardner will be Mrs. Laurelwood's friend, a friend obviously beneath her, but a friend who will render her the homage which will assuage the disappointment her marriage has brought. "There was something, too, about the expedition that appealed to her sense of fitness—a nice English family setting out together to a nice English farm, where another nice English family, conveniently inferior in rank, welcomed them and waited on them" (222). As Mrs. Laurelwood cannot achieve her sense of importance from her own creative actions (as her actions as wife and mother are dictated by the class to which she belongs), she needs the welcome and the service of the Lardners to help her achieve a sense of self worth.

Although Mrs. Lardner supplies a "not very distinguished conversation," she gives her "all that her heart" needs of "kindly deference and homely scandal" (227). The reason these talks are enjoyable is that they "never came anywhere near the secrets at the bottom of her heart," because "there could never be any question of her taking into her confidence a woman so comfortingly different from herself in speech and ways and class. Mrs. Lardner would not expect it" (227). She remembers with embarrassment a chat with a woman of her own class which had "ended up in painful confidences about her husband and the unforgivable statement that all men were the same" (227).

In her conversations with Mrs. Lardner, Mrs. Laurelwood can keep up a facade. She does not have to be honest with herself; she does not have to face the painful facts about her life with her husband. She can bask in the supposed adulation of the woman of lower class and maintain her own self-esteem, instead of finding her selfhood in her own honest reactions to the life she finds a disillusionment.

When she becomes upset over her husband's friendship with Mrs. Brown, it is Mrs. Lardner she goes to, to "soothe away this strange, new uneasiness which had made her even afraid of Idolsfold." She feels "like a child who has fallen down and frightened herself," and Mrs. Lardner is the "nurse who would pick her up and dust her and tell her she wasn't hurt" (242). And she is not disappointed, for "her emotions had been translated from her own concerns into another world, and her distaste for Mrs. Brown's goings on was now nearly as impersonal as Mrs. Lardner's. With Mrs. Lardner she sat in judgment on a world to which she did not belong" (244). The thought that she need not judge her own world is comforting.

But even though she convinces herself that she does not belong to the world of the Lardners and the Mrs. Browns, she actually shares that world, for her husband and Mrs. Brown are acting in a manner beneath their class. The children's nurse, Nanny, provides some of the same comfort found in Mrs. Lardner, for when with her, she experiences "that relief from pretense and strain which accompanied an escape out of her own class" (247). Although she can give up the "pretense and strain," she must remember that she must give away no part of herself. With these women, her inferiors, she can act a satisfying role. She can live the role of a satisfied upper class lady, knowing that her authenticity as a person will never be questioned. These two, who believe themselves to be beneath her, look up at the person presented to them, never questioning that person's reality.

Mr. Laurelwood also knows that their circle of upperclass friends does not satisfy his need for friendship. He tells his wife that they don't know anyone " 'who isn't dull and ignorant and conventional,' " just as they are themselves. He adds that they have their own " 'dreary little circle of people who don't know the first things about art—or literature or music' " (251). He decries the "tattle of ignorant people like the Lardners, who've built up this preposterous scandal around a woman who dares to be different from what they think a clergyman's wife ought to be" (251). Mr. Laurelwood can transcend his own class values by finding values which transcend all classes in the artistically creative. He can see both the boorishness of the upper class and that of the lower class. Mrs. Brown attracts him because she has some knowledge of painting, because they have a common interest. And she is not afraid to transgress social mores to act freely, even though she gets herself talked about by both classes. But he is not free to pursue a friendship with Mrs. Brown.

When Mrs. Lardner suggests a favorite remedy of her own class, a confrontation, and Mrs. Laurelwood cannot live with the disappointment in her husband's eyes when Mrs. Brown accedes to her request and does not appear for tea, Mrs. Laurelwood blames herself, but it is for the wrong reason. "The longer he held her the deeper the roots of her penitence seemed to go, stabbing down beneath this episode of Daisy Brown, right down through all the faults and fusses of family life . . . right down to the bitter soil of that first married night at Idolsfold, where all his present disappointment seemed to lie in the first failure of her love" (276). Because she could not accept her husband as he was (and a Victorian wife might be hard pressed to accept the sexual side of marriage, ill-prepared as she was), she had to build up a facade instead of a real marriage. This facade covered not only her relationship with her husband, but also her relationship with the Lardners. The one time when she confided in Mrs. Lardner about her suspicion of her husband and Mrs. Brown was the one time she allowed herself to relate to Mrs. Lardner as woman to woman. But she knows that experience will never be repeated. "Was it because once they had met as sister women instead of as Mrs. Lardner and Mrs. Laurelwood? Frances did not know. All she knew was that she did not want to talk to Mrs. Lardner any more—or ever again" (227).

When she knows that she will never return to Idolsfold, she should have "woken to sadness, reluctance, regret," but instead, she woke "with a curious lightness of heart" (278). She need never fear again that rending of the facade. She can go back to her life, conventional and unexciting, but a life in which the pain of authentic emotion need never again appear.

In presenting the class struggle through the relationship of the Lardners and the Laurelwoods, Sheila Kaye-Smith points out the difficulties involved for people who feel themselves to be above or below other people because of the societal class structure. Just as Dick Lardner cannot move out of his class to embrace the rewards which the upper class could provide, so Mr. Laurelwood cannot move out of his class to embrace the rewards he would have found satisfying in a society of "different" people, artistically creative.

The failure of a society to allow each individual to reach his or her own creative powers can be experienced through *The Lardners and the Laurelwoods.* Yet, aside from a few penetrating insights into the snobbishness of the upper class, Sheila Kaye-Smith does not condemn or praise either class. Each has its weaknesses; each its strengths. And each contributes, through individual insecurity, to keep the division wide. Each individual has his or her own abilities and must find proper outlets for them. When the individual fails to do so, in this novel because of the class structure, the person fails to reach his or her potentiality as a creative being. The necessity of relying on class for one's self-esteem means that one relies on a shaky foundation. No one in the novel achieves a measure of maturity, except Bess, but then, Bess rejects the class structure at an early age and compensates by making herself believe in her superiority over the Laurelwoods. She can accept the return of the Laurelwoods because she has convinced herself that she is actually better than they. Only when the truth about how the family regards her and her family is painfully made clear does she react with the decision that no longer will the family be welcome. The buried psychological hurt, even though compensated for, rises briefly to the surface. Through the separation of the classes, neither class gains; both classes lose. But in the game played, Sheila Kaye-Smith reveals the truth about the players.

V   Mrs. Gailey

Rosamund Gailey (*Mrs. Gailey,* 1951) resembles Dick Lardner in her perception of the good inherent in the upper class. But although Dick perceives the aesthetic values of the society, Rosamund perceives its material values. She also resembles Susan Spray and Joanna Godden in that she is a woman trying to make a satisfactory life in a society which limits her ability to act in freedom of its convention. Like Susan Spray, she must satisfy a weak ego; like Joanna Godden, she must satisfy her emotional needs. But even though there are similarities between Rosamund Gailey and the other characters referred to, her story reveals a different facet of personality, and the class struggle takes on a different hue than that in the other novels.

Rosamund Gailey appears as an individual who is both good and bad. An analysis of her desires and the means through which she attempts to achieve them sheds some light on the psychological needs which, depending on the means taken to satisfy them, bring either satisfaction or destruction to the individual. Joanna Godden's life brought her to maturity; Susan Spray's brought her to destruction as a person; Dick Lardner's left him his values, but destroyed his value to his society. Rosamund Gailey is held back by her place in society (as is Joanna Godden); she tramples on her better instincts to rise in this society (as does Susan Spray); and she destroys her value to society (as does Dick Lardner). Her choice, although it satisfies an emotional need, destroys the commitment which, like Joanna Godden's, might have brought her to full maturity.

Mrs. Rosamund Gailey, a widow in her late thirties, comes to Doleham Manor to act as secretary to Lesley Bullen, an ungainly young woman whose nonconformity with the expectations of polite society are the bane of her mother's existence. Iris Winrow, her mother, a devotee of the conventions existing before World War II, chooses to live in London rather than at Doleham Manor, in order to avoid her daughter and her daughter's unconventional lifestyle. Lesley, as inheritor of Waters Farm, one of the farms belonging to Doleham Manor, has taken poor people to live at the farm, somewhat in the manner of a commune, with the purpose of training them to be farmers.

Mrs. Winrow takes an intense dislike to Mrs. Gailey, as she recognizes her desire to ingratiate herself with the household for her own selfish purposes. She takes every opportunity to humiliate her, and she treats her like a servant. Lesley, on the other hand, becomes friends with Mrs. Gailey, sympathizing with her because of her difficult life, which includes supporting a twelve year old retarded son, Michael. Michael lives with Mrs. Gailey's mother.

At Doleham Manor, Mrs. Gailey falls in love with Bob Hightower, Lesley's departing secretary, a man of unsavory character. She meets him secretly. The meetings compensate for her unexciting life as Lesley's secretary. Noticing that Lesley appears to be attracted to one of her mother's tenant farmers, Charley Vine, Mrs. Gailey encourages the relationship for two reasons. One is to help Lesley achieve a satisfactory marriage, and the other is to humiliate Mrs. Winrow through Lesley's marriage to a man of the lower class. Charley Vine had been a major in World War II. His education and his experience equal or surpass Lesley's, but Mrs. Winrow can only see his inferior class status. The Vines wish to buy Birdskitchen, the farm they have been working as tenants, but Mrs. Winrow, although she needs the money, is loathe to sell, because in her eyes this would artificially raise their social status.

Mrs. Gailey encourages Lesley to invite Charley Vine to the Red Cross Ball. At the ball, mistaking his interest for love, Lesley falls in love with him. But Lesley does not know that Charley has been courting a young woman for many years and is only waiting for his family to acquire Birdskitchen before proposing to her. When she finds out the true state of affairs, Lesley's humiliation is too much for her to bear. Also, she knows that, having found out about her daughter's interest in Charley Vine, her mother will never agree to the sale of the farm. Because of her unhappiness, Lesley steals Mrs. Gailey's bottle of sleeping pills and commits suicide. She had made a will the day before in which she leaves Waters Farm to the people who live on it and the rest of her estate, several thousand pounds, to Mrs. Gailey. To her mother, she leaves her forgiveness.

Mrs. Gailey gives the money to Bob Hightower to enable him to buy passage for them both to New Zealand. She leaves her mother and her son and goes to a new life in a new country with Bob Hightower.

VI   *The Attempt to Climb*

As can be seen, the plot is a slight one. The conflict rages between Mrs. Winrow and Mrs. Gailey, primarily. Both Lesley and Charley Vine are emotionally unconscious of the difference in class which divides Mrs. Winrow and Mrs. Gailey, but both are very much aware of the outward effects that stepping out of class brings. Had Charley's interest not been engaged elsewhere, undoubtedly he and Lesley could have had a very satisfactory life together. The story hinges primarily on Mrs. Gailey's struggle for upward motion and Mrs. Winrow's struggle to keep her in her place.

Underneath their outward facade, Mrs. Winrow and Mrs. Gailey are very much alike. Both are hypocrites. Both are widowed, Mrs. Winrow doubly. Mrs. Gailey's husband, Phil, had given her a taste of what upper class life might be like, although he himself was a wastrel, while both of Mrs. Winrow's husbands had allowed her to experience completely the life of ease and selfishness of the upper class. Both struggle; Mrs. Winrow to preserve herself from the encroachment of inferiors who attempt to be her equal, and Mrs. Gailey to break through the social barricade which prevents her from achieving a comfortable life.

Iris Winrow's dislike of Rosamund Gailey comes instantaneously the first time she sees her, for she "thoroughly disliked the looks of the new secretary. She was common—not a lady. . . . She looked neither immaculate nor discreet."[12] Rosamund recognizes the antagonism, realizing that she has failed "for some reason to recommend herself to that snooty old bitch" (8), even though she has tried with all her charm to do so. Mrs. Winrow's "smile was a part of that duty of charm in which she had been brought up" (1), but the smile is not for the new secretary. Rather it is for the stationmaster whose aid she needs. Thus both women endeavor to use an outward charm to cover an inward need, hypocritically pretending to an emotion neither feels.

Like Mrs. Winrow, Mrs. Gailey has cultivated charm, not because she had been brought up to its cultivation, but because with it she covers her lack of ability. She "depended less on her typing than on her gift for making people like her." She knows that she "mustn't let Mrs. Winrow make her lose her confidence in that pleasant manner which for so long had kept her in jobs she might otherwise have lost for lack of skill" (9). And she must make money, not only for herself, but also to support Michael, her son. Michael is "all she had" (16).

Also like Mrs. Winrow, she is motivated by snobbishness. When she toys with the idea of making herself attractive to Charley Vine, she catches herself up, for

a farmer's son was useless. He had shed no luster and he could offer no escape into that world which she had viewed with such longing from its soiled fringes—the world of which Phil had given her a glimpse and which ever since she had been determined to enjoy. Yet there had been nothing about him to tell her he did not belong to that world. She felt almost angry with him for being so unlike her idea of a farmer's son. (22)

Thus she wishes, like Mrs. Winrow, that the classes keep the division between them. She desires only to climb up from her class (and Charley Vine's) into the class of the Mrs. Winrows and the Lesley Bullens.

While Mrs. Winrow and Mrs. Gailey are exactly alike in their class consciousness, Lesley is very different. Lesley, product of a mother who "always makes" her feel "more stupid" than she is (23) and a father who didn't like her because she wasn't a boy, feels an intense social awareness of the plight of the less fortunate. She feels that luxury is wrong when so many struggle for the bare necessities of life. Her lifestyle, geared to helping these unfortunates, enrages her mother, as does Lesley's failure to conform to the upper class dress code and her failure to marry.

Lesley's second cousin, Nicholas Cheynell, feels that it is because Lesley herself is " 'a sort of social misfit' " that she can empathize with " 'other social misfits,' " and " 'she's so idealistic that she thinks she's only got to show them kindness and generosity in order to get the best out of them in return' " (30). But Nicholas Cheynell fails to see the rest. Naturally soft-hearted, Lesley cannot bear to see others in want. She has a genuine love for her fellow creatures. She also lacks the hypocrisy which results in feeling that her class makes her a notch above the farmers and workers, while at the same time she bends to their aid. She truly feels herself equal to the rather riff-raffy lot at Waters Farm. She has an inner security and independence of feeling which give her courage to defy her mother and mold her life into its own pattern.

And Lesley's innate goodness affects Mrs. Gailey. Her kindness to her and her empathy with her when she learns of Michael bring Mrs. Gailey to an "embarrassment which only one other person in the world could make her feel. Only Michael could pull her up like this with a sudden jerk of compunction. She had the strange feeling that Lesley was at her mercy just as Michael was, made vulnerable by innocence" (42). She can give way to her authentic emotions when confronted by innocence—of her son and of Lesley. These two do not threaten her, as the lack of innocence of people out for their own advantage in a harsh world threatens her. She must put up a front of willing service, of friendliness, of pleasing mien to mask her inner feeling of self-loathing. But with these innocents, these who accept her at face value, Michael and Lesley, she can be the person she was meant to be.

Because Lesley accepts Rosamund Gailey, genuinely likes her, she can even pity Lesley. "The wiles that had failed so notably with Iris Winrow had won an easy success with her daughter, and had in consequence ceased to be wiles. Rosamund quite genuinely liked her employer, her liking being all the stronger for an admixture of contempt. It was pleasant, it did her good, to be able to look down on a girl in so much better circumstances than she was—better born, better bred, better off, better educated, and yet withal completely cuckoo" (82). Just as the child Bess can like Meg because she can have a feeling of superiority over her, so Mrs. Gailey can like Lesley. In both cases the feeling of inferiority engendered by class must be compensated for by the feeling of contempt for the member of the upper class.

Mrs. Gailey's power over people resides in her ability to make them like her. Through this ability, she can make people do her will or refuse to do theirs. This gift is her

stock in trade, her only fortune. . . . Mrs. Winrow not only disliked her, she despised her, she saw through her, she exposed her even to herself. She had made her feel a miserable little upstart woman without abilities, manners, or looks, who made her way through life by toadying and flattering her betters, but yet had never really succeeded in getting anywhere and would never really succeed. In other words, Mrs. Winrow had made her feel unsure of herself; and, as she had no one but herself to rely on, that was a blow at the whole substance and security of her life. (82)

Mrs. Winrow stands, then, as her alter ego, as the person she dislikes most because she is the person she is most like. She is every bit as snobbish as Mrs. Winrow, but she does have a chance at a saving grace in her genuine love for both Michael and Lesley. Through her own struggle, she can feel somewhat the struggle (suffering) of others. Mrs. Winrow, on the other hand, never having had to struggle, remains almost completely unaffected by her daughter's tragedy and has no feeling at all for the plight of the Vines in losing their farm.

Yet Mrs. Gailey, "in spite of her friendship with women who had their roots in a class above her, in spite of twelve years of marriage to the outcast son of a good family . . . still felt most at ease with those whom she would have liked to consider her inferiors" (84). Thus she can relate to those with whom she can be honest, with those with whom she can be herself. Taught by her society to respect and look up to the upper class, she cannot rid herself of the idea that people of this class are better than she. Yet, while aspiring to be one of this class, she needs the people she can be herself with—people of her own class. She is betrayed by her insecurity.

With Michael and with Lesley, she can also be herself. She can even, for a moment, forget her revenge on Mrs. Winrow and think "only of the happiness her scheme would bring to a girl of whom she was growing really fond" (102). For although a "marriage between Lesley Bullen and Charley Vine would completely wipe out the mounting score of insult and exposure," such a marriage would "do Lesley herself all the good in the world" (86). In like manner, when Charley Vine asks her about her little boy, he sees her "turn into a real person" (102).

Forced through her reliance on them to associate with the poor wastrels at Waters Farm, Mrs. Gailey realizes that there is another level to the class to which she belongs.

She had fallen into a world below that which she normally inhabited, even below the world in which she was born. This was something quite different from the relaxation she had found in talking to servants, who had only taken her back to her own beginnings. Her present company, with its shameless morals and manners, its spiv talk, its dirty crowding around a table spread with newspapers and laid with tine, would have been despised as an underworld in her mother's neat kitchen. . . . The Turners bore the same relation to her own respectable working-class origin as Phil Gailey had borne to the society of Doleham Manor and Pookreed. They showed her how far she could fall. (215)

And fall thus far she does. The learned response to those of her own class, coupled with the attraction of Bob Hightower, vanquish her newly made resolution. As she cannot find her selfhood, her sense of identity as a person in her own accomplishments, she attempts to find it in Bob Hightower. She had a chance at self-fulfillment through Lesley's friendship, but after Lesley's death, her strength is diminished. She knows well that her life with Bob represents uncertainty at best and degradation at worst. Betrayed by her need for self-verification (even the verification of an unscrupulous Bob Hightower), she "could no more stop herself doing what she had begun to do than she could have stopped a brakeless, driverless car rushing downhill" (309).

As she kisses Michael before leaving him, perhaps forever, she feels "a catch in her throat," and she rushes out "followed by the sound of her mother's crying and the humming of his top" (310). Although there is the pain of loss of her daughter with knowledge of the hardship this will bring to both her and her grandson, her mother's crying symbolizes not only her pain on the knowledge of the kind of life her daughter will live, but the tears for what she could have been. The humming of Michael's top reminds Mrs. Gailey of the innocence which might have been her salvation. Could she have maintained the sense of self brought forth by innocents such as Michael and Lesley, could she have sacrificed her life to the nurture of her son, she could have left behind her own insecurity. But the insecurity can now only be assuaged by a sense of belonging to an attractive man, even though the man is not worthy of her devotion.

Both Mrs. Winrow and Mrs. Gailey are motivated by an insecurity, which forces them to find their importance outside themselves—Mrs. Winrow in class consciousness and Mrs. Gailey, when she cannot achieve a higher class, in a love affair. Mrs. Winrow's snobbishness leads her to reject not only the social-climbing Mrs. Gailey, but also her own daughter. Because Lesley cannot enhance her mother's position by making a suitable marriage, she must be rejected and made to feel "stupid." When Anne Cheynell listens to Mrs. Winrow's plans for leaving, after Lesley's suicide, "it almost seemed as if, under all the mourning veils, Lesley's death was a relief—no awkward, shambling figure who would not mix with her guests . . . who managed to look badly dressed in the latest model of a Paris house, who never seemed to like well-bred, well-behaved people, but attached herself only to social misfits" (284).

Although Mrs. Winrow can now live without the embarrassment of having a daughter such as Lesley, she in no way blames herself for Lesley's despair. She comforts herself with the belief that Mrs. Gailey, by encouraging Lesley to seek out Charley Vine and for introducing her to sleeping pills, has caused Lesley's death. She feels no responsibility, for she lives in a world in which doing the acceptable thing has replaced doing the right thing. The responsibility her daughter took on all too willingly, that of being her brother's and sister's keeper, Mrs. Winrow completely rejects. Even Lesley's will, leaving her mother her forgiveness and Mrs. Gailey the entire amount of her money, fails to make her see her part in Lesley's death.

She is described by Charley Vine as the type of person who insists on "clinging to a state of things that's over and done with" (205), afraid there won't be anything left if the remnants of their pride in class are taken away. Condemned by her lack of vision to remain like "a post firmly fixed among its changing waters" (89), Mrs. Winrow cannot see that the old order changes. Social barriers are crumbling.

But the old order can be seen to change, as Lesley's bequest to Mrs. Gailey represents her affection for one she considers her equal, her friend. Mrs. Gailey can rise to Lesley's height because she knows that Lesley both accepts and respects her, which in turn allows her to accept and respect herself. With Lesley's death, this strong prop to Mrs. Gailey's self-esteem vanishes. Paradoxically, Lesley's bequest to her becomes the instrument, not of a further rise of Mrs. Gailey to maturity, but the means through which she begins to sink to the level of the Turners. Without the bequest, she would not have been asked to accompany Bob Hightower to New Zealand.

The change in class structure may be seen through the ideas of Charley Vine, who determines to combine both the old and the new, keeping the best of both upper and lower class. "His life should be like the new Birdskitchen, built upon the old, keeping the framework, but modernized, enlarged, improved" (110). The old, narrow life of his father cannot satisfy him. "Ever since his return from Germany he had missed those contacts with a more sophisticated world which he had enjoyed out there—the dances, the theaters, the cocktail parties. . . . He wasn't going to look down on his father's friends of the sort of folk he'd always known. But the world was wider nowadays; you could know all sorts, and social barriers were breaking down under the weight of dangers and adventures shared alike by all" (111).

Charley Vine, through his education and his army experience, has seen that people differ, not because of class, but because of their own individuality. He tells his father that he gave his son these ideas with his education, which enabled him to serve in the army as an officer. As he met people of all classes, he could fit in with them, just as his father should. But Charley realizes the difficulty of change for his parents when he thinks of his mother as a young girl,

in domestic service, being courted by the son of a struggling tenant farmer, and having to wait years before they could afford to marry, and then to work hard for many more years to keep their home and educate their son. All their lives the Manor folk, as they called them, had been a separate breed, people of a different, more fortunate race than themselves. Neither their struggle nor their prosperity had any real connection with them that they could see, and now they had no standard to judge them by, for how did they know that the rules of their own good sense and kindly feeling prevailed at Doleham? (113)

And, of course, their own good sense and kindly feeling do not prevail at Doleham, for even before she found out about Lesley's interest in Charley Vine, Mrs. Winrow was reluctant to sell Birdskitchen to the Vines, for she did not want "farmers" for neighbors.

Sheila Kaye-Smith does not, then, as believed by Pendry,[13] insist on the incompatibility of the classes. Rather, she recognizes the strength and weakness of individuals, a recognition which transcends class structure. Both Mrs. Winrow and Mrs. Gailey, of opposite classes, are strong advocates of class structure; both are hypocrites. Both Lesley Bullen and Charley Vine are strong advocates of equality; both are moral people. Michael Cheynell, although born into the upper class and, as such, an adherent to its rights, shows himself to be honest and just in his fight to gain Birdskitchen for the Vines. The class system, as an institution, vanquishes the Vines. Despite anything they can do, despite anything Michael Cheynell can do on their behalf, the Vines must submit to the will of the landlord, Mrs. Winrow.

Those like Lesley and Charley, who have security in their own worth, do not need to rely on class structure to provide self-worth. The insecure Mrs. Gailey, however, torn both by her inner needs for recognition and her insecure financial situation, needs to maneuver into a position of importance. She cultivates the servants at the manor, not only because she feels more herself with them, but because she can add to her material comforts through the gin and cigarettes they steal for her from their employer.

Mrs. Gailey remains both a victim of, and a champion of, the class system, even though her proximity to the Turners and her marriage to Phil Gailey show her that there are levels within each class. As victim of a class system which strips her of a feeling of self-worth, she must compensate by ingratiating herself with those she considers her superiors. She must also manipulate them, where possible, to gain power over them. She champions the class structure by attempting to climb into it, in the expectation that she will enhance both her own self-image and her material well-being. In this, she resembles somewhat Susan Spray, whose dual motivation led her to a self-glorification and to material wealth.

There appears one false note, however, in the characterization of Mrs. Gailey, even though, on the whole, she appears to be a person torn by conflicting good and bad emotions. This false note resides in her relationship with Bob Hightower. Motivation for her attraction to Bob Hightower is lacking. The reader is told not much more than that she is attracted to wastrels. It remains difficult to imagine, however, that the shrewd Mrs. Gailey cannot twist Bob Hightower to her desires, as she twists others. Perhaps Miss Kaye-Smith reiterates the idea given in her other stories (notably *Joanna Godden* and *Susan Spray*) that women are betrayed by their emotions, which overpower both good sense and morality. In *Mrs. Gailey*, however, additional motivation for action would enhance the plausibility.

Nevertheless, Mrs. Gailey remains an outstandingly interesting character, primarily for the contradiction in her character, which makes her at the same time love and despise Lesley and hate and emulate Mrs. Winrow. The class struggle shows forth, not so much as struggle between classes, but rather as a struggle between members of each class who need to rely on the false valuation they find in membership in the upper class.

The human need which keeps classes separated appears clearly in both *The Lardners and the Laurelwoods* and *Mrs. Gailey*. This need has its basis in the struggle for ego satisfaction. Class structure, according to Miss Kaye-Smith, becomes another false prop for the falling ego. But optimism remains in her images of the class structure, for this structure gives way before love, which recognizes no class barrier. When love becomes universally achieved, class structures will inevitably fall. The message is optimistic; and the message is Christian.

CHAPTER 7

Final Estimate

PERHAPS the life work of Sheila Kaye-Smith might best be
summed up by the remark of Hugh Walpole that "it has been
Sheila Kaye-Smith's virtue . . . to make her novels timeless."[1]
Because she probes the psychological depths of human needs,
she presents characters who appear as real people, caught up in
forces which either aid or hinder them in their growth toward
human maturity. The human needs which form these forces do
not change with changes in a societal view. The need for
acceptance as an individual, the need for freedom to reach one's
potentiality, the need for community with one's fellow human
beings—all these reside deep within human nature. By showing
the basis for these human needs and by picturing the constructive or destructive use to which they are put, Sheila Kaye-Smith
provides insight into the core of life—human relationships.

Ample evidence exists that her novels were extremely popular
in their time. Unfortunately, other techniques and other visions
supplanted the solid, expert, professional technique wedded to a
hopeful vision that remained central to the talent of Sheila Kaye-
Smith. But copies of her books are still available in libraries, and
apparently they are read. Many should be reprinted, and not
only because they are good stories, but because they provide
insight into this time and every time.

Sheila Kaye-Smith always tells a good story. From the time she
was a tiny girl, stories were part of her. Her imagination pulled
together memories, observations, and intuitions, resulting in
artistry. Her stories contain well-plotted action as well as
expertly motivated characters. The effect is to draw the reader
into the circle of which she writes, so that the characters step
from the printed page into the reader's consciousness.

As was pointed out, Miss Kaye-Smith's critical acclaim rests on
her use of Sussex as locale, her conversion to Roman Catholicism,

and her supposed ability to write like a man. But each novel can be taken as an entity. The locale, the religion, the objectivity, the power, the breadth of vision—all serve to point to a vision which sees life in a certain way. This way is based in part on the tragic vision, in which each individual brings about his or her own destruction through a tragic error. Added to this is the Judeo-Christian tenet, in which love of self and love of neighbor must be manifest before maturity as a human being can be reached, plus an existential view of existence in which action precedes essence, so that her protagonists become by doing. Added to these fundamentals is a questioning of them, particularly in the characterization of Reuben in *Sussex Gorse*. Although she does not take sides in the struggle of her protagonists for selfhood against the formidable forces arraigned against them, she conveys the idea that good and evil depend upon sanctions outside the individual. When a character fails to accept these sanctions, which are rooted in love, he or she falls, in her view, even though he or she may see himself or herself as successful, as, for example Reuben Backfield and Susan Spray.

Thus, there is paradox in her characterizations as there is in life. She has no easy answers to the problem of existence. But, then, Sheila Kaye-Smith does not attempt to write religious tracts. She presents stories based on human need, and she succeeds in making this need understandable to her readers. To read *Sussex Gorse* and *Tamarisk Town* is not only to experience the effect of a driving ambition, but also to understand the need through which this driving ambition comes into being as well as the lack of moral/ethical considerations which helps create the human monster. *Joanna Godden* and *Susan Spray*, although stories of women, have no propaganda to preach. The reader can find in these women characteristics which pertain to both sexes. The contradictions which make up human existence can be experienced through reading *The End of the House of Alard* and *The View from the Parsonage*. And most important of all, that which keeps the human race apart, instead of together in community, can become part of one's consciousness through reading *The Lardners and the Laurelwoods* and *Mrs. Gailey*.

The other novels of Sheila Kaye-Smith are likewise important and satisfying to the reader, because all pertain in some way to the struggle all human beings must engage in as part of a growth to maturity. Although there are certain basic principles of human activity which appear important to Miss Kaye-Smith and although she writes of a certain locale, all of the novels are different. Even though the theme may be similar in two or more novels, as pointed out above, a different view of the conflict brings added insight into the struggle.

Despite the fact that some critics complain of a certain detachment in her writing, this detachment is fortunate because it allows her to write with an objectivity which would not be possible if she clearly supplied her own value system. This is not to say that there are no moral/ethical values present in the novels. As noted above, her vision is based upon traditional values of Western culture. Yet her objectivity allows the reader room to interpret motivation, development, and conclusion based on his or her own values, provided, of course, that these values generally agree with the traditional values as noted above.

Sheila Kaye-Smith appears to have lived a happy and productive life. She created herself through her writing and through her acceptance of the religion of which she felt herself part. The creation of self appears as an important aspect of her novels. Undoubtedly her awareness of this as the fundamental goal of every human being underlay not only her novels, but her life as well. The self she created shows forth in her autobiographical works as well as in her novels. She did not wear her religion on her sleeve, but the values she apparently lived by and the values that appear in her novels are those basic Judeo-Christian ones whose core is the creative power of love.

Sheila Kaye-Smith has enhanced English literature, not only by preserving a section of England for immortality, but also by preserving fundamental human values which might help her readers in their own creation of self. For this she deserves their gratitude.

Notes and References

Chapter One

1. *Three Ways Home* (New York, 1937), p. 14.
2. *Ibid.*, pp. 13–14.
3. *Ibid.*
4. *Ibid.*, p. 16.
5. *Ibid.*, p. 18
6. *Ibid.*, pp. 7–8.
7. *Selina* (New York, 1935), p. 16.
8. Those who believe that only parents can (or should) raise children might find in these stories accounts of upbringing by a nurse or nanny which resulted in children free to grow in a secure, loving atmosphere, without having to bear the burden of parental neuroses.
9. G. B. Stern, "Sheila Kaye-Smith," in *And Did He Stop and Speak to You?* (London, 1958), p. 78.
10. *Selina*, p. 64.
11. G. B. Stern, "Sheila Kaye-Smith," *Books on Trial*, XIV (March 1956), 285.
12. Edward Wagenknecht, *Cavalcade of the English Novel* (New York, 1947), p. 561.
13. W. Gore Allen, "Sheila Kaye-Smith: Convert Novelist," *Irish Ecclesiastical Record*, 5th ser., LXIX (June 1947), 520–521. Allen develops an interesting parallel between her novels and her spiritual convictions at the time of her writing them.
14. *Three Ways Home*, p. 255.
15. Wagenknecht, p. 561. This idea is further developed in Chapter 4 of this study.
16. *All the Books of My Life* (New York, 1956), pp. 26–27. An interesting account of Miss Kaye-Smith's school day appears here. "The day started with prayers at nine, at a quarter to eleven there was a short recess, and the school broke up finally at a quarter to one, so the pupils—or students as they were officially called—could hardly be considered over-driven. Those who liked could return to the college in the afternoon for an hour and a half's 'preparation,' but it was thought better for me to spend my afternoon out of doors and do my homework later. Even in the sixth form this was not supposed to take more than

two hours, so it may be said that learning was less of a rod than a wand waved lightly over me." p. 26.

17. *Three Ways Home*, p. 7.
18. *Ibid.*, p. 3.
19. *Ibid.*, pp. 53-55, *passim.*
20. *Ibid.*, pp. 58-59.
21. *Ibid.*, pp. 58-59.
22. *Ibid.*, pp. 62-63.
23. See Wayne Booth, *The Rhetoric of Fiction* (Chicago, 1969).
24. *Three Ways Home*, pp. 64-65.
25. *Ibid.*, p. 65.
26. "Publisher's Note," *The Tramping Methodist* (New York, 1922), p. vii.
27. *Ibid.*
28. *Three Ways Home*, p. 69.
29. *Ibid.*, p. 66.
30. *Ibid.*, p. 65.
31. *Ibid.*, p. 67.
32. *Ibid.*, p. 68.
33. *Ibid.*
34. *Ibid.*, p. 71.
35. *Ibid.*, p. 73.
36. *Ibid.*, pp. 78-79. Miss Kaye-Smith continues with an analysis of her progression toward conversion, which, although interesting, is not pertinent to the focus of this study.
37. *Ibid.*, pp. 81-82.
38. *Ibid.*, p. 86.
39. *Ibid.*, p. 90.
40. *Ibid.*, p. 83. An interesting and detailed account of Miss Kaye-Smith's reading is found in her *All The Books of My Life*.

Chapter Two

1. Elizabeth A. Drew, *The Modern Novel: Some Aspects of Contemporary Fiction* (Port Washington, New York, 1967), p. 129. This work was originally published in 1926.
2. *Sussex Gorse* (New York, 1916), p. 25. All further references to this novel in this chapter will be indicated by page number in parentheses in text.
3. Robert Thurston Hopkins, *Sheila Kaye-Smith and the Weald Country* (London, 1925), pp. 131-32.
4. There is an interesting description of the region of which Boarzell Moor is part in "The Old Forest," *Times Literary Supplement* (London), November 13, 1953, p. 729. Part of it is as follows: "The Weald is a coherent region unto itself, so complete as almost to be

comparable to a human artifact, such as a bowl or a vase." It is the "great basin between the North and South Downs which stretches roughly from the Dover Coast westward into Hampshire. It is not flat, for along the middle of it runs a spine of hills, lower than the Downs, but high enough to rise above the frost line."

5. As pointed out above, Boarzell Moor is bound to call up to the reader's imagination Thomas Hardy's Egdon Heath *(The Return of the Native)*. But while Egdon Heath provides atmosphere and effect, Boarzell Moor provides motivation.

6. Hopkins, p. 135.

7. Malcolm Cowley, "The Woman of Thornden," *Dial*, LXVIII (February 1920), 259.

8. Hopkins, pp. 133–34. See reference to relationship between Sheila Kaye-Smith's and Hardy's use of place above.

9. It is interesting to note that Henry James wrote to A. C. Benson in 1896: " 'But I have the imagination of disaster—and see life as ferocious and sinister!' " (as quoted by Lionel Trilling in *The Liberal Imagination*, [New York, 1976], p. 60). Trilling writes: "What James saw he saw truly, but it was not what the readers of his time were themselves equipped to see. That we now are able to share his vision required the passage of six decades and the events which brought them to climax. Henry James in the eighties understood what we have painfully learned from our grim glossary of wars and concentration camps, after having seen. . .human nature laid open to our horrified inspection." p. 60. Sheila Kaye-Smith shared the prescience of Henry James as she "laid open to our horrified inspection" the monstrous character, Reuben.

10. *Tamarisk Town* (London, 1919), p. 1. All further references to this novel in this chapter will be indicated by page number in parentheses in text.

11. Anne Morrow Lindbergh recognizes this liberating power of love. She writes: "to be deeply in love is, of course, a great liberating force and the most common experience that frees—or seems to free— young people. The loved one is the liberator. Ideally, both members of a couple in love free each other to new and different worlds." "Introduction," *Hour of Gold, Hour of Lead: Diaries and Letters, 1929–1932* (New York, 1973) p. 1. Mrs. Lindbergh goes on to talk about her own experience: "I was no exception to the general rule. The sheer fact of finding myself loved was unbelievable and changed my world, my feelings about life and myself. I was given confidence, strength, and almost a new character. The man . . . believed in me and what I could do, and consequently I found I could do more than I realized, even in that mysterious outer world that fascinated me but seemed unattainable. He opened the door to 'real life' and although it frightened me, it also beckoned. I had to go." Ibid. Reprinted by permission.

12. "Tamarisk Town," *Times Literary Supplement* (London), September 1919, p. 472.

13. See Soren Kierkegaard's discussion of the three stages of life; the aesthetic, ethical, and religious in such works as *Either/Or (Princeton, 1944)* and *Philosophical Fragments* (Princeton, 1962).

Chapter Three

1. W. L. George, "Sheila Kaye-Smith," in *Literary Chapters* (Boston, 1918), p. 94.

2. Andrew E. Malone, "Sheila Kaye-Smith: A Novelist of the Farm," *Living Age,* CCCXXIII (November 15, 1924), 388.

3. Mother M. Agatha, "Contemporary Catholic Authors: Sheila Kaye-Smith of Sussex, an Appreciation," *Catholic Library World,* LXXV (November 1943), 36.

4. Cornelius Weygandt, *A Century of the English Novel* (New York, 1925), p. 189.

5. Una Stannard, *Mrs. Man* (San Francisco, 1977), pp. 50-51.

6. Norman Mailer once said that he wrote with his penis. (Stannard, p. 50).

7. Elaine Showalter, *A Literature of Their Own: British Women Novelists from Bronte to Lessing* (Princeton, New Jersey, 1977), p. 90.

8. An enlightening analysis of this sexist criticism is made in Showalter and in Stannard.

9. In this study, the use of the terms "feminine" and "masculine" reflects the labels of society, rather than the acceptance of these to denote an innate difference (except physically) between the sexes.

10. Apparently this is the only one of Sheila Kaye-Smith's novels which has been made into a motion picture. A postproduction shooting script with full dialogue, music, sound effects, and action continuity is in the collection of the New York Public Library. The script is marked, "London, 1947."

11. Hopkins, p. 177.

12. Drew, p. 128.

13. *Ibid.,* p. 129.

14. J. R. N. Maxwell, "Sheila Kaye-Smith," *America,* January 10, 1939, p. 339.

15. Agatha, p. 35.

16. Margaret Mackenzie, "The House That Sheila Built," *Thought,* VI (June 1931), 113.

17. Fletcher Allen, "Sheila Kaye-Smith In and Out of Fiction," *The Literary Digest International Book Review,* September 1924, p. 726.

18. G. B. Stern, "The Heroines of Sheila Kaye-Smith," *Yale Review,* XV (October 1925), 204.

19. Patrick Braybrooke, "Sheila Kaye-Smith and Outlook," *Some*

Catholic Novelists: Their Art and Outlook (London, 1931), p. 197.

20. *Ibid.*, p. 191.

21. The place names are authentic. Various novels mention the same place. Marlingate is "Tamarisk Town."

22. Although Sheila Kaye-Smith wrote a long short story continuing Joanna Godden's Story (*Joanna Godden Married and Other Stories* [New York, 1926]), the continuation disappoints and does not add to the characterization given Joanna in the novel. It has therefore been omitted in this analysis of *Joanna Godden*. Sheila Kaye-Smith does not think much of the sequel and says, "The novel itself had ended on such an uncertain note that several readers had written to ask for a sequel. . . . I did not feel equal to writing another novel about Joanna—my novels are dead selves which, as a rule, I have small inclination to revive. But the idea of a story of thirty thousand words appealed to me. . . . Unfortunately, I found it impossible to think of her still as she had been in the novel. . . . The critics . . . reasonably objected that the continuation of her story is flat and thin in comparison with its lustier beginnings" (*Three Ways Home*, 191-92).

23. *Joanna Godden* (New York, 1922), p. 17. All further references to this novel in this chapter will be indicated by page number in parentheses in text.

24. The ceremonial opening of a door has apparently taken on a heavy symbolic meaning. When challenged to become feminists (those who work for equality between the sexes), many of my women students protest that they "want a man to open the door" for them.

25. *Susan Spray* (New York, 1931), p. 3. All further references to this novel in this chapter will be indicated by page number in parentheses in text.

Chapter Four

1. *Three Ways Home*, p. 99.

2. *Ibid.*, p. 100.

3. *Ibid.*, p. 105.

4. *Ibid.*, p. 108.

5. *Ibid.*, p. 113.

6. *Ibid.*, p. 114.

7. *Ibid.*, p. 118. Miss Kaye-Smith had been to hear Mass in a Roman Catholic church in order to assess her response to the Catholic Mass.

8. *Ibid.*, pp. 120-21.

9. *Ibid.*, p. 122.

10. *Ibid.*, p. 128.

11. *Ibid.*, p. 131.

12. The manuscript of *Tamarisk Town* in the Berg Collection, New

York Public Library is "copiously corrected. Considerable passages are
sometimes cancelled in a general reduction of text. Also shown is a ten-
page outline of the story . . . which seems to be a careful plotting of
the story before rather than a resume after the fact. It shows how
carefully Sheila Kaye-Smith planned her way, for the novel develops
almost exactly as pre-arranged." (John D. Gordan, "Novels in
Manuscript; An Exhibition from the Berg Collection," *New York Public
Library Bulletin*, LXIX [June 1965], 408.) This is an indication that
Sheila Kaye-Smith accepted the advice of her friend, George Moore—
"Willy George," as she called him—that she must carefully plan her
stories.

13. *Three Ways Home*, pp. 137-42. The present writer does not
consider *Green Apple Harvest* one of her best books, although it is a
very good one. For this reason, it was not selected for analysis. If space
were unlimited, one could profitably analyze all of the novels.

14. *Ibid.*, pp. 146-47, *passim.*
15. *Ibid.*, p. 148.
16. *Ibid.*, p. 150.
17. *Ibid.*, p. 151.
18. *Ibid.*, p. 152.
19. *Ibid.*, p. 153.
20. *Ibid.*, p. 154.
21. *Ibid.*, p. 159.
22. *Ibid.*, p. 167.
23. *Ibid.*, p. 173.

24. Coulson Kernahan, writing in 1925, notes that "admirers of her
novels are counted by hundreds of thousands, how many of
those. . .know even that she has published two slender volumes of
poetry?" (Sheila Kaye-Smith As a Poet," *The Nineteenth Century*,
XCVII [June 1925], 910. Kernahan refers to *Willows Forge and Other
Poems* (1914) and *Saints in Sussex* (1923). She also published another
volume of poetry, *Late and Early* (1931). Apparently *Saints in Sussex*
was worked over and republished in 1926.

25. *Three Ways Home*, p. 177.
26. *Ibid.*, p. 179.
27. *Ibid.*, p. 191.
28. *Ibid.*, p. 193.
29. *Ibid.*, pp. 207-09, *passim.*
30. *Ibid.*, p. 222.
31. *Ibid.*, p. 224.
32. *Ibid.*, p. 226.
33. *Ibid.*, pp. 230-31.
34. *Ibid.*, p. 232.
35. *Ibid.*, p. 235.
36. *Ibid.*, p. 237.

37. *Ibid.*, p. 253.

38. *Ibid.*, p. 255.

39. Stern, *And Did He Stop and Speak to You?*, p. 83.

40. "Miss Kaye-Smith, a Novelist Dead," *New York Times*, January 15, 1956, p. 21.

41. *Ibid.*

42. "Jane Austen's World: Two Women Novelists Talk," *The Times Literary Supplement*, January 8, 1944, p. 21.

43. *Kitchen Fugue* (New York, 1945), p. 1.

44. Stern, *And Did He Stop and Speak to You?*, p. 79.

Chapter Five

1. Raymond Mortimer, "New Novels," *The New Statesman*, September 8, 1923, p. 621.

2. A. J. Dawson, "The Passing of the County Family," *The Bookman*, LXIII (October 1923), 40.

3. Mortimer, p. 621.

4. Dawson, p. 40.

5. F. Allen, p. 733.

6. Mary Stack, "Sheila Kaye-Smith Now," *Commonweal*, XXI (January 18, 1935), 335.

7. Gilbert Keith Chesterton, as quoted in title page, *The End of the House of Alard* (New York, 1923).

8. *The End of the House of Alard*, p. 4. All further quotations from this novel in this chapter will be indicated by page number in parentheses in text.

9. See Albert Speer, *Inside the Third Reich* (New York, 1970), translated from the German by Richard and Clara Winston.

10. Patrick Braybrooke, *Some Goddessess of the Pen* (London, 1927), Index Reprint Series, Books for Library Press, Inc., (Freeport, New York, 1966), p. 15.

11. *The View from the Parsonage* (New York, 1954), p. 1. All further quotations from this novel in this chapter will beindicated by page number in parentheses in text.

12. W. G. Allen, p. 526.

13. *Ibid.*, pp. 527–28.

Chapter Six

1. James W. Tuttleton, *The Novel of Manners in America* (Charleston, North Carolina, 1972), p. 7.

2. Tuttleton writes: "By a novel of manners I mean a novel in which the manners, social customs, folkways, conventions, traditions, and mores of a given social group at a given time and place play a

dominant role in the lives of fictional characters, exert control over their thought and behavior, and constitute a determinant upon the actions in which they are engaged . . ." (p. 10). He defines society as "the structure of 'Classes,' cliques, or groups by which specific American communities are organized" (p. 13). Although referring to American novels of manners, undoubtedly he would include, even with greater emphasis, specific British communities in his definition.

3.   Reference here is to the British television series, *Upstairs, Downstairs,* presented by PBS.

4.   Tuttleton, p. 262.

5.   *Ibid.*, p. 272.

6.   *Ibid.* Although Tuttleton refers primarily to American society, his ideas are valid for British society as well, perhaps even more so, as classes have always been more definitely defined in Britain than in America.

7.   John P. Marquand's novels, also, focus on the problems brought about by class expectations. See the present writer's doctoral dissertation: *"Elements of Greek Tragedy in the Novels of John Phillips Marquand."* (St. John's University, Hillcrest, New York, 1962). Note particularly the analysis of *The Late George Appley, H. M. Pulham, Esquire,* and *Sincerely Willis Wayde.* James W. Tuttleton has a chapter on Marquand in his book referred to above.

8.   E. D. Pendry, *The New Feminism of English Fiction* (Tokyo, 1956), p. 59.

9.   *The Lardners and the Laurelwoods* (New York, 1947), p. 2. All further quotations from this novel in this chapter will be indicated by page number in parentheses in text.

10.   See May Sarton, *As We Are Now* (New York, 1973). This is a novel based on a similar theme, in which the protagonist is an elderly woman.

11.   Donald Brook, *Writers' Gallery* (London, 1944), pp. 80–81.

12.   *Mrs. Gailey* (New York, 1951), p. 4. All further quotations from this novel in this chapter will be indicated by page number in parentheses in text.

13.   Pendry, *The New Feminism of English Fiction.*

Chapter Seven

1.   Hugh Walpole, "Sheila Kaye-Smith," in *Sheila Kaye-Smith. A Biographical Sketch, Some Critical Appreciations and a Bibliography* (New York and London: Harper's, 1929), p. 7. This small publication is available in the New York Public Library at 42nd Street.

Selected Bibliography

PRIMARY SOURCES

1. Novels

The Tramping Methodist. New York: E. P. Dutton & Company, 1922. First published in 1908.
Starbrace. New York: E. P. Dutton & Company, 1926. First published in 1909.
Spell Land. New York: E. P. Dutton & Company, 1927. First published in 1910.
Isle of Thorns. New York: E. P. Dutton & Company, 1913.
The Three Furlongers (Three Against the World). Philadelphia and London: L. B. Lippincott & Company, 1914.
Sussex Gorse. New York: Alfred A. Knopf, 1916.
The Challenge to Sirius. London: Nisbet & Co., Ltd., 1917.
Little England. London and New York: Cassell and Company, Ltd., 1919. Also published under the title *The Four Roads*.
Tamarisk Town. London and New York: Cassell and Company, Ltd., 1919.
Green Apple Harvest. New York: E. P. Dutton & Company, Inc., 1921.
Joanna Godden. New York: E. P. Dutton & Company, Inc., 1922.
The End of the House of Alard. New York: E. P. Dutton & Company, 1923.
The George and the Crown. New York: Harper and Brothers, 1924.
Iron and Smoke. London: Cassel and Company, Ltd., 1928.
The Village Doctor. New York: E. P. Dutton & Company, Inc., 1929.
Shepherds in Sackcloth. London: Cassell and Company, Ltd., 1930.
Susan Spray. New York and London: Harper & Brothers, 1931. Published in England under the title *The History of Susan Spray, the Female Preacher*.
The Children's Summer. London: Cassell and Company, Ltd., 1932. Also published as *Summer Holiday*. New York: Harper & Brothers, 1932.
Gipsy Waggon. New York and London: Harper & Brothers, 1933. Also published under the title *The Ploughman's Progress*.
Superstition Corner. New York and London: Harper & Brothers, 1934.
Gallybird. New York: Harper & Brothers, 1934.

163

Selina (Selina Is Older). New York and London: Harper & Brothers, 1935.

Rose Deeprose. New York and London: Harper & Brothers, 1936.

The Valiant Woman. New York and London: Harper & Brothers, 1936.

Ember Lane. New York: Harper & Brothers, 1940.

The Secret Son (The Hidden Son). New York: Harper & Brothers, 1942.

Tambourine, Trumpet, and Drum. New York: Harper & Brothers, 1943.

The Lardners and the Laurelwoods. New York and London: Harper & Brothers, 1947.

The Happy Tree (The Treasures of the Snow). New York: Harper & Brothers, 1949.

Mrs. Gailey. New York: Harper & Brothers, 1951.

The View from the Parsonage. New York: Harper & Brothers, 1954.

2. Short Stories

Joanna Godden Married. New York and London: Harper & Brothers, 1926.

3. Poetry

Willows Forge and Other Poems. London: E. Mcdonald, 1914.
Saints in Sussex. Birmingham: Elkin Mathews, Ltd., 1923.
Songs Late and Early. London: H. Hamilton, 1931.

4. Autobiographical Works

Three Ways Home. New York and London: Harper & Brothers, 1937.
Kitchen Fugue. New York and London: Harper & Brothers 1945.
All the Books of My Life. New York: Harper & Brothers, 1956.

5. Miscellaneous

Samuel Richardson. London: Regent Library, 1911.
John Galsworthy. London: Nisbet & Co., 1916.
The Mirror of the Months. New York and London: Harper & Brothers, 1925.

DOYLE, PAUL A. "Sheila Kaye-Smith: An Annotated Bibliography of Writings About Her." *English Literature in Transition,* XV:3 (1972), 189–98. Lists, with annotation, all the critical material on Sheila Kaye-Smith, completely and authoritatively. Gives the most

important facts from each item listed. Represents the single, most
excellent publication on Sheila Kaye-Smith.

———. "Sheila Kaye-Smith," *English Literature in Transition*, XVI:2
(1973), 152–53. Continues the above bibliography.

———. "Sheila Kaye-Smith," *English Literature in Transition*, XVII:1
(1974), 45–46. Continues the above bibliography.

———. "Sheila Kaye-Smith," *English Literature in Transition*, XVIII: 1
(1975), 62. Continues the above bibliography.

SECONDARY SOURCES

ALLEN, W. GORE. "Sheila Kaye-Smith: Convert Novelist." *Irish
Ecclesiastical Record*, 5th ser., LXIX (June 1947), 518–28.
Discusses the relationship between Sheila Kaye-Smith's novels and
her religious conversion.

DREW, ELIZABETH A. *The Modern Novel: Some Aspects of Contemporary
Fiction*. Port Washington, New York: Kennicot Press, 1967
(originally published in 1926), pp. 115–16, 124–32, and *passim*.
Reveals insight into Sheila Kaye-Smith's craft in the depiction of
energetic and vital characters.

HOPKINS, ROBERT THURSTON. *Sheila Kaye-Smith and the Weald Country*.
London: Cecil Palmer, 1925. Relates actual places to the setting of
the novels. Gives some synopsis and analysis of selected novels,
always relating them to scenes of the Weald country.

MACKENZIE, MARGARET. "The House That Sheila Built." *Thought*, VI (June
1931), 108–18. Compares the house that Sheila Kaye-Smith lived
in during her later life with some of her novels. Gives some insight
into selected novels and stresses the enduring quality of her work.

MALONE, ANDREW E. "Sheila Kaye-Smith: A Novelist of the Farm." *Living
Age*, CCCXXIII (November 15, 1924), 387–90. Stresses her
likeness to Thomas Hardy in her objectivity and frankness in the
depiction of farm life.

SHOWALTER, ELAINE. *A Literature of Their Own: British Women Novelists
from Bronte to Lessing*. Princeton, New Jersey: Princeton University Press, 1977. Documents the adverse criticism given women
novelists simply because they were women and therefore believed
to be inferior writers.

STANNARD, UNA. *Mrs. Man*. San Francisco: Germainbooks, 1977. Discusses
the effect on women of a culture that expected women to be the
lesser part of their husbands.

STERN, G. B. "The Heroines of Sheila Kaye-Smith." *Yale Review*, XV
(October 1925), 204–208. Discusses her heroines in comparison
with her heroes. Analyzes specifically Morgan Wells of *Tamarisk
Town* and Joanna Godden.

————. "Sheila Kaye-Smith." In *And Did He Stop and Speak to You?*
    London: Regnery, 1958. Gives a synopsis of her life, particularly
    her early life and her collaboration with G. B. Stern in writing
    about Jane Austen.
TUTTLETON, JAMES W. *The Novel of Manners in America.* Charlotte,
    North Carolina: The University of North Carolina Press, 1972.
    Gives a detailed view of the connection between the novel and the
    class structure of society.

Index

Agatha, Mother M., 58
Allen, Fletcher, 58, 94
Allen, W. Gore, 20, 121
Anglicanism contrasted with Roman Catholicism, 112-13
Apollonian, 44
Austen, Jane, 26, 92
Aylward, Reverend A. Frewen, 94

Battle of Britain, 92
Bishop Kaye, 17
Blake, William, 26
Booth, Wayne, 22
Borrow, George, 26
Braybrooke, Patrick, 58, 111
Briareus, 48
Bronte, Emily, 26, 87

Chesterton, Gilbert Keith, 88, 98
Church of England, 86
Civil War, 85
Cowley, Malcolm, 34

Dante, *Divine Comedy*, 21
Dawson, A. J., 94
de La Condamine, Robert (Sheila Kaye-Smith's grandfather), 18
Dionysian, 44, 46, 58
Drew, Elizabeth, 29, 57
Dublin Review, 88

Fielding, Joseph, 26
Fry, Reverend F. Penrose, 89

Greek tragedy, 31, 111

Hardy, Thomas, 27, 34, 95; *The Mayor of Casterbridge*, 42; *The Return of the Native*, 27; *Tess of the D'Urbervilles*, 34

Hitler, Adolph, 40, 93, 111
Hopkins, Robert Thurston, 34, 57

Irish Ecclesiastical Record, 20

James, Henry, 157n9
Jane Eyre, 40

Kaye, Sir John, *History of the Indian Mutiny*, 17
Kaye-Smith, Sheila: ancestry, 17-18; Anglicanism, 90; Anglo-Catholicism, 85, 87, 88, 89, 91, 94; attempt to climb, 143-51; birth, 18; "Catholic" novels, 91; Catholicism, 86, 88, 89, 91, 107; childhood, 19-21; the chosen of God, 72-84; Christian message, 151; Church of England, 89; class struggle, 151; clergyman's wife, 89, 90-91; conversion to Anglo-Catholicism, 107; conversion to Roman Catholicism, 90-92, 113, 121, 152-53; creation and destruction of self, 43-55; creation of self, 28-41, 154; creative power of love, 154; death, 93; early life and influences, 17-19; early novels, 21-24; education, 20-21; emergence of self, 60-70; final estimate, 152-54; goals, 21; Hastings, 18; human maturity, 152, 153; human relationships, 152; human values, 154; innocence and evil, 115-23; Italy, 90; Judaic-Christian values, 112, 153, 154; keeping one's place, 128-31; later life and later novels, 85; liberating power of love, 157n11; life at Doucegrove, 90, 91, 92-93; The Literary Agency of London, 21;

167

local reputation, 24-25; London, 89; loss of beauty, 132-36; loss of love, 136-41; love and duty: religion and convention, 97-112; man-like attitude, 56, 153; marriage, 89-90; "masters", 26; the matter of class, 124-25; pen name, 21; Platnix, 19; reading, 25-26; religion, 18; religion and family, 94-95; religious conversions, 93; religious influence, 18; return to religion, 86-87; Roman Catholicism, 18, 21, 22, 89; St. Leonards, 18, 19, 89; St. Leonards Ladies' College, 20; school days, 155-56n16; story-telling, 19-20; struggling women, 56-59; Sussex novelist, 18; Victorian society, 19; Who's Who, 92; women characters, 58; women's suffrage, 24

WORKS:
All the Books of My Life, 93, 155n16
Challenge to Sirius, The, 85-86, 93, 94
Children's Summer, The, 19, 20, 89, 91-92
End of the House of Alard, The, 87, 88, 91, 93, 94, 95-113, 122-23, 124, 153
Gallybird, 91
Green Apple Harvest, 58, 86, 87
Iron and Smoke, 89
Isle of Thorns, 26
Joanna Godden, 57, 58, 59-70, 86, 87, 88, 124, 150, 153
Joanna Godden: The End of the House of Alard, 87-89
Joanna Godden Married, 89
John Galsworthy, 93
Kitchen Fugue, 93
Lardners and the Laurelwoods, The, 17, 107, 125-41, 153
Little England, 85, 86, 93
Mirror of the Months, The, 93
More Speaking of Jane Austen, 93
Mrs. Gailey, 17, 125, 141-51, 153
Rose Deeprose, 20, 92
Saints in Sussex, 89
Samuel Richardson, 93

Selina, 19, 20, 89
Selina Is Older, 92
Shepherds in Sackcloth, 89, 90
Speaking of Jane Austen, 92, 93
Spell Land, 25, 26, 94
Starbrace, 20, 23, 26, 56
Superstition Corner, 91, 107
Susan Spray, 22, 57, 70-84, 91, 95, 124, 150, 153
Sussex Gorse, 26, 27-41, 43, 46, 55, 56, 58, 60, 85, 86, 94, 95, 124, 153
Tamarisk Town, 18, 41-55, 60, 85, 86, 87, 88, 94, 95, 124, 153, 159-60n12
Three Against the World, 26
Three Ways Home, 18, 22, 91, 93
Tramping Methodist, The, 20, 21, 22, 23, 26
View from the Parsonage, The, 90, 93, 95, 112-23, 124, 153
Village Doctor, The, 19, 89

Kipling, Rudyard, 34

Lindbergh, Anne Morrow, Hour of Gold, Hour of Lead: Diaries and Letters 1929-1932, 157n11

Macbeth, 29
MacFarquhar, Miss (Sheila Kaye-Smith's grandmother), 18
Mackenzie, Margaret, 58
Mailer, Norman, 158n6
Martindale, Reverend C. C., 88, 91
Maxwell, J. R. N., 58
Milton, Collected Poems, 21
Moore, George, 87
Mortimer, Raymond, 94
Mrs. Man, 158n5
Mussolini, 93

Nietzsche, 25
Novel of manners, 124-25, 161-62

Oedipus, 29, 53
Olympic deities, 48

Pendry, E. D., 125, 149
Pride and Prejudice, 61
Protestantism, 91

Richardson, Samuel, 26
Roman Catholicism contrasted with Anglicanism, 112–13

Showalter, Elaine, *A Literature of Their Own*, 158n7
Smollett, Tobias, 26
Speer, Albert, 111
Stack, Mary, 94
Stannard, Una, *Mrs. Man*, 158n5
Stern, Gladys (G. B. Stern), 20, 92, 93
Sterne, Lawrence, 26
Sussex, 34, 88, 89, 90, 93, 95, 152–53
Swedenborg, Emanuel, 25

Times Literary Supplement, 54

Titans, 48
Tuttleton, James W., 124, 161–62

Vanity Fair, 61
Victorian heroine, 70
Victorians, 56

Wagenknecht, Edward, 20
Walpole, Hugh, 152
Weald, The, 156–57
Wessex, 95
Weygandt, Cornelius, 56
Women's struggles, 84
World War I, 85
World War II, 93, 136
Wuthering Heights, 40